Watergate and Investigative Journalism

Kristin Thiel

Cavendish Square

New York

Published in 2019 by Cavendish Square Publishing, LLC
243 5th Avenue, Suite 136, New York, NY 10016

Copyright © 2019 by Cavendish Square Publishing, LLC

First Edition

No part of this publication may be reproduced, stored in a retrieval system, or transmitted in any form or by any means—electronic, mechanical, photocopying, recording, or otherwise—without the prior written permission of the copyright owner. Request for permission should be addressed to Permissions, Cavendish Square Publishing, 243 5th Avenue, Suite 136, New York, NY 10016. Tel (877) 980-4450; fax (877) 980-4454.

Website: cavendishsq.com

This publication represents the opinions and views of the author based on his or her personal experience, knowledge, and research. The information in this book serves as a general guide only. The author and publisher have used their best efforts in preparing this book and disclaim liability rising directly or indirectly from the use and application of this book.

All websites were available and accurate when this book was sent to press.

Library of Congress Cataloging-in-Publication Data

Names: Thiel, Kristin, 1977- author.
Title: Watergate and investigative journalism / Kristin Thiel.
Description: First edition. | New York : Cavendish Square Publishing, 2018. |
Series: The Fourth Estate: Journalism in North America | Includes bibliographical references and index.
Identifiers: LCCN 2017061449 (print) | LCCN 2018006379 (ebook) |
ISBN 9781502634887 (eBook) | ISBN 9781502634870 (library bound) |
ISBN 9781502634894 (pbk.) | ISBN 9781502634900 (6 pack)
Subjects: LCSH: Investigative reporting--United States--History--20th century--Juvenile literature. |
Investigative reporting--United States--History--21st century--Juvenile literature. |
Watergate Affair, 1972-1974--Press coverage--Juvenile literature.
Classification: LCC PN4888.I56 (ebook) | LCC PN4888.I56 T45 2018 (print) | DDC 070.4/309730904--dc23
LC record available at https://lccn.loc.gov/2017061449

Editorial Director: David McNamara
Editor: Caitlyn Miller
Copy Editor: Nathan Heidelberger
Associate Art Director: Amy Greenan
Designer: Christina Shults
Production Coordinator: Karol Szymczuk
Photo Research: J8 Media

The photographs in this book are used by permission and through the courtesy of:
Cover and throughout the book, (torn newspaper) STILLFX/Shutterstock.com;
p. 4 UPI/Bettmann/Getty Images; p. 9 United Press/Library of Congress/File: Joseph McCarthy. jpg/Wikimedia Commons/Public Domain; p. 13 H. J. Myers/Library of Congress/File: Nellie Bly 2.jpg/ Wikimedia Commons/Public Domain; p. 18 Underwood Archives/Archive Photos/Getty Images; pp. 22-23 Open Media Ltd./File: Jessica Mitford appearing on "After Dark, 20 August 1988.jpg/Wikimedia Commons/CCA-SA 3.0 Unported; p. 26 Steve Northup/The LIFE Images Collection/Getty Images; pp. 28, 42, 47, 92-93 Bettmann/Getty Images; p. 34 Tasos Katopodis/Getty Images; p. 37 CBS Photo Archive/ Getty Images; p. 39 PhotoQuest/Archive Photos/Getty Images; p. 45 Warner Bros./Moviepix/Getty Images; p. 50 The Washington Post/Getty Images; p. 53 Ronald S. Haeberle/The LIFE Images Collection/ Getty Images; p. 55 Library of Congress/Corbis/VCG/Getty Images; pp. 56-57 Owen Franken/Corbis/Getty Images; p. 59 Hill Street Studios/Blend Images/Getty Images; p. 61 Wally McNamee/Corbis/Getty Images; p. 63 Oliver F. Atkins (1917–1977)/Nixon Presidential Materials Project/File: Nixon leaving whitehouse. jpg/Wikimedia Commons/Public Domain; p. 69 Jim Watson/AFP/Getty Images; p. 74 Frederick M. Brown/ Getty Images; p. 79 Alex Gotfryd/Corbis/Getty Images; pp. 82-83 Kathryn Osler/The Denver Post/Getty Images; p. 85 AP Images.

Printed in the United States of America

CONTENTS

1 A Golden Age of Investigative Journalism 5

2 The Storytellers 27

3 Watergate's Stories 51

4 Investigative Journalism Half a Century After Watergate 75

Chronology 96

Glossary 98

Further Information 100

Bibliography 103

Index 109

About the Author 112

Carl Bernstein (*left*) was twenty-nine and Bob Woodward (*right*) was thirty when the *Washington Post* won a Pulitzer Prize for its Watergate coverage.

A Golden Age of Investigative Journalism

Watchdog journalism. Accountability reporting. Muckraking. Over the years, investigative journalism has been associated with a lot of terms. At a high level, investigative reporting simply means in-depth reporting. Investigative journalists dive deep to explore a topic, and this work usually sheds light on wrongdoing. Investigative journalists are interested in exposing corruption and abuse of power at the highest levels of corporations, governments, and militaries. These journalists want to affect people's perspectives. They want to encourage people to rise up and demand that wrongs be corrected. They also want to change the behavior of the wrongdoers. That may mean a change in public policy or a legal ruling against a person or corporation.

Wrongdoing always exists, but the popularity of investigative journalism in the United States has come and gone over the decades. It can be seen prominently at the country's founding, when the colonies were splitting from Britain. Investigative journalism appears again during the early 1900s, when the country was growing into the modern, industrialized superpower it is today. That is often considered the first golden age, or peak time, of investigative journalism. Watergate, in the early 1970s, is named as the start of its second golden age.

Watergate was a political scandal in the early 1970s. It led to Richard Nixon's resignation, the only resignation of a president in US history. A major event such as this can make investigative journalism popular. If a story unfolds or develops over time, like Watergate did, there is reason for journalists to keep investigating. The story holds people's attention, and the public wants updates.

However, the public has to be open to learning the secrets that investigative journalists uncover for the journalists' work to be effective. In times of peace, people may not care to know that anything negative is happening. On the other hand, sometimes society feels unstable, maybe because of war or social or economic injustices. At such times, people are more interested in understanding the people and events behind the instability. Watergate happened during a time of upheaval in the United States. It also involved a president who was already under suspicion for abusing his power.

Finally, for investigative journalism to be effective, there must be media outlets that can share stories widely. During Watergate, these outlets were newspapers, magazines, radio, or television. Part of the reason investigative journalism was not common in the 1800s was that towns and cities in the United States were more spread out. Technology and transportation did not exist that could share news across places. The news people cared about, and had access to, was local only. Watergate happened during a more modern era, when people were more connected across the entire country. Television news was born. That put stories in every home with a newfound immediacy. It did not lead the Watergate reporting, but it did eventually play a role in it. Television news outlets covered the Watergate hearings, for example. The hearings were held by a special Senate committee investigating what wrongdoings may have occurred. These hearings, the presentation and analysis of evidence, led to Nixon's resignation. According to the Museum of Broadcast Communications, television coverage of the hearings greatly increased the public's awareness of Watergate. It also led to a lot of unique cooperation among news channels. The television networks worked together to share responsibility for coverage of the hearings.

"Investigative reporting in America did not begin with Watergate," Leonard Downie Jr. writes in a *Washington Post* editorial. He worked for the *Washington Post* for forty-four years, including as its executive editor. He was an investigative journalist during the Watergate scandal, a story that *Washington Post* reporters Bob Woodward and Carl Bernstein broke. But, he continues, investigative journalism "became entrenched in American journalism—and has been steadily spreading around the world—largely because of Watergate." Watergate and investigative journalism are inextricably connected. The scandal has had a lasting effect on journalism and journalists. However, Watergate was not the first example of investigative journalism, nor has it been the last.

Early Investigative Journalists

Briefly, the first time investigative journalism in the United States had much influence was in the early 1900s. All the ingredients needed for its existence were present then. There were scandals, an interested public, and technology capable of spreading the news. "Muckraking" was a term used for investigative journalism then. It is particularly important to understand this period of journalism. Later, during the Watergate era, many journalists continued to be called "muckrakers." Some even called themselves by that name.

President Theodore Roosevelt introduced the word to the public when he used it in a speech in 1906. He meant it in a negative way. The United States was experiencing growing pains. It was entering an exciting period of new industries and new wealth. With that came disparity: there was a growing financial and social gap between business and government leaders and everyone else. Muckrakers did not celebrate the people in charge. Instead, they exposed the hardship that big business was causing.

Muckrakers made Roosevelt's life more complicated, but he could appreciate their well-meaning challenges to authority. He even met regularly with muckrakers like Sinclair Lewis, who wrote *The Jungle*. Lewis's book exposed the dark side of the increasingly industrialized food industry. It looked at the lives of people, mostly immigrants, who worked in newly industrializing cities, like Chicago, in new businesses like big-factory meatpacking. Newspaper, magazine, and book exposés of the time led to changes like the creation of the Food and Drug Administration, to make food safer; the start of the popular election of the Senate, to make representation fairer; and the start of government trust-busting, or the breaking up of business monopolies. As the book *The Journalism of Outrage* explains, President Roosevelt

Journalism in the 1950s was shaped by McCarthyism, named after Joseph McCarthy.

A Golden Age of Investigative Journalism 9

eventually contacted Lewis's publisher and said, "Tell Sinclair to go home and let me run the country for awhile." To challenge a leader to do better such that his or her work was disrupted would be one of the highest compliments an investigative journalist could receive.

Journalism in the 1950s and 1960s

The 1950s saw the beginning of another major wave of change in the United States. It swept across culture, politics, and technology, changing everything in big ways. Young people began experimenting with new freedoms. Women's rights and civil rights turned into movements that would only grow bigger over the next few decades. The Cold War between the United States and the Soviet Union heated up. The Red Scare, or McCarthyism, was part of this. This was an anticommunist crusade by Americans against Americans suspected of being communists.

People were open to change in ways they had never been before. New technology made it possible for ideas to spread and for people to come together more easily. This was the perfect atmosphere in which journalism could also change and journalists could break important stories, like Watergate.

The changes of the 1950s intensified in the following decade. The election of a passionate young man, John F. Kennedy, as US president encouraged citizens to speak out against injustices. After Kennedy was assassinated in 1963, that activism continued. After Kennedy's death, people were motivated not out of a feeling of hope but out of one of disillusionment. They still wanted a better world—they were just angrier about it. Technology continued to improve. Social movements in support of civil rights continued to grow. War continued to cost lives and tap American resources as the United States joined the Vietnam War. People, including journalists, pushed back against authority. Reporters began to realize that a lot of the pieces of information they were being fed were not facts but versions of facts. The information was spun in favor of the person or group distributing the information.

New Journalism

New Journalism grew out of the 1960s. This form of reporting combines journalistic research with fiction's storytelling techniques. Some of the new journalistic forms of this era were new nonfiction journalism and precision journalism, alternative journalism and counterculture journalism, and advocacy journalism. New nonfiction journalism and precision journalism focused on setting, plot, sounds, feelings, and dialogue. They are literary, like a novel or short story, but also factual. Truman Capote and Tom Wolfe are two writers who are known for this form. Alternative journalism and counterculture journalism express a distinct point of view and usually speak out against the mainstream power structure. Advocacy journalism supports political and social reform. Gloria Steinem, for example, could be considered an advocacy journalist.

The rise of New Journalism shows that people in the 1960s and 1970s were hungry for truth from their news sources. New Journalists "were contributing to a wider discussion of the nature of truth," *Encyclopaedia Britannica* explains. Mainstream journalists, including investigative reporters, "echoed" New Journalism's argument that "objectivity does not guarantee truth and that so-called 'objective' stories can be more misleading than stories told

Nellie Bly: One of the First Female Investigative Journalists

In the late 1800s, Nellie Bly was doing what women in their twenties were not usually allowed to do at that time in the United States. She was working as an investigative journalist.

Bly was born Elizabeth Jane Cochran on May 5, 1864, in Cochran's Mills, Pennsylvania. She and her hometown shared a name because her father founded the town. Unfortunately, he died unexpectedly, and the family was left with nothing. Bly tried to help support them. She enrolled in college to become a teacher. When costs became too high, she dropped out. Then, she and her mother ran a boarding house together. Bly had dreams beyond managing a hotel, and she made those dreams come true through writing.

A local newspaper published an editorial that said that women should get married and stay at home. Bly wrote an angry response. The editor of the newspaper was impressed with her work and hired her. This was when Bly took her pen name. "Nelly Bly" was a popular song that celebrated marriage and housekeeping. Bly was making a joke and a point by taking her "Nellie" outside the home to work. Bly continued writing about women's rights. She even went undercover to write about women working in sweatshops.

She is famous for posing as a patient in a mental institution in New York. She did this to expose the terrible conditions

Nellie Bly sat for this photo around 1890.

patients lived with. Bly's exposé was reprinted as a book, *Ten Days in a Mad-House*, in 1887.

Though she retired from journalism when she got married at age thirty, she returned to work when she was fifty-five. She wrote about the women's suffrage movement, among other stories, until her death at age fifty-seven.

from a clearly presented personal point of view." In 1983, Steve Weinberg, then president of the group Investigative Reporters and Editors, said investigative journalism did not have to be only about uncovering illegal activities. It could be "in-depth, explanatory reporting." This hearkens back to the New Journalism of the 1960s and 1970s. By 1996, the Society of Professional Journalists would drop "be objective" from its ethics code. Instead, the group urged "fairness" and "accuracy." Quite simply, the era of New Journalism has led to an ongoing interest in media that seeks and speaks the truth.

It is also important to mention New Journalism because it helps to distinguish the styles of two of the most famous investigative journalists of the Watergate era, Bob Woodward and Seymour Hersh. Woodward helped break the Watergate story for the *Washington Post*. Hersh led the *New York Times*'s Watergate team. Bill Kovach, former editor of the *New York Times*'s Washington bureau, talked with the *Guardian* in 2004 about Woodward and Hersh. Hersh had just published a book about US military actions after the September 11 terrorist attacks. "[Woodward] has become the diarist of sitting administrations," Kovach said, "and [Hersh] has continued to be the muckraker. [Hersh] continues his outrage, and [Woodward] has become the recorder of the official story in Washington." Woodward's style is a bit more literary in its reliance on detail (and thus more representative of New Journalism), as opposed to Hersh's more "old-fashioned" style. Both strive to tell the truth after much detailed research, but their styles can fall on opposite sides of the spectrum.

Support for Investigative Journalism

In the 1960s, support for investigative journalism came from a couple of big directions. In 1964, the Pulitzer Prize, which offers some of the premier journalism awards, started recognizing excellent investigative reporting. That same year, the Supreme Court decision in *New York Times v. Sullivan* made it difficult for public officials to successfully sue the press for libel. This helped journalists feel safer reporting the truth, even if it would damage the reputation or career of a powerful public official. The Freedom of Information Act, passed by Congress in 1966, made it much easier for reporters to find vital information. The new law required the executive branch of the federal government to make information available, without question or argument, if a citizen (such as a journalist) asked for it. The law made room for certain exceptions, however, including for information classified due to national security.

The New News: Television

By the late 1950s, about 90 percent of Americans had a television. For the first time, journalists writing for newspapers and magazines were worried about their jobs. Television was a new, exciting medium in the country. People were starting to get their news from it, instead of from print.

Cartoons in the *Quill* made observations about this phenomenon. The *Quill* is the magazine of the Society of Professional Journalists, which at the time was called Sigma Delta Chi. The organization was for all types of journalists, but the cartoons focused on the perspectives of print journalists.

Some cartoons made fun of journalists who worked for television news. One from December 1958 is captioned, "Never wastes a second—he shaves, comments on the news and gives the commercial, all at the same time." According to a review of these cartoons in *Slate*, this showed "a contrast between appearance-centric TV news people and earthy, even disheveled, print reporters." A cartoon from April 1959 shows a television news anchor singing, dancing, and playing a guitar. "He's too imaginative to be confined to the usual method of newscasting," reads the caption. This cartoon implies that television is all about gimmicks. It is style over substance. It is about how it superficially looked and sounded and not about the content.

Of course, television was not going away, and it had its benefits. Even in its early years, it supported investigative journalism by providing another publishing outlet for in-depth stories. The three commercial television networks of the time, ABC, CBS, and NBC, expanded their prime-time evening news shows from fifteen to thirty minutes starting in 1963. They did this to make room for investigative documentaries.

Investigative Journalists of the 1950s and 1960s

Because of the world events of the 1950s and 1960s, the public was more willing to receive a big story of government corruption by the time Watergate happened. They had come to understand that there was turbulence in world affairs. Because of new technology, news was able to spread easier and faster across the country. This, too, would support the spread of Watergate coverage. Finally, the individuals working in the media in the 1950s and 1960s were important forbearers of those who would report on Watergate.

The journalists who came immediately before Woodward and Bernstein set the stage in a way that directly supported Woodward and Bernstein's courageous and dogged pursuit of information. The following reporters were three of the ones who took advantage of their situation and leveraged changing technology to bring new kinds of hard-hitting stories to the public. Partly because of their work, Woodward and Bernstein could react the way they did when Watergate happened.

Edward R. Murrow

Edward R. Murrow was a well-known radio journalist when the transition to television began. In 1935, CBS hired him, and he was assigned to London. He did not know he was moving to what would soon be a war zone.

From late 1939 to early 1940, the first months of World War II, Murrow reported on the bombing of London. He transmitted his stories from rooftops. By doing so, he became the first reporter to include the sounds around him in his stories. He was not reading the news in a quiet studio. This made the war feel very real to listeners in the United States. Poet Archibald MacLeish said at the time that Murrow "burned the city of London in our houses and we felt the flames that burned it."

Even though Murrow was initially uncomfortable with television, he made the switch. He knew he had to in order to keep an audience for the news stories he believed were important. In 1951, his show *See It Now* debuted. He tackled one of the biggest stories of the time: anticommunism. US citizens were being encouraged to turn against anyone they suspected of being a communist. In 1953, Murrow told the story of a soldier discharged from the military because his family had reported him as possibly being a communist.

The child of a prisoner of war watches President Richard Nixon announce that American troops will leave Vietnam.

The Vietnam War's Effects on Journalism

The Vietnam War was between North Vietnam and its allies and South Vietnam and its allies, which included the United States. The United States was directly and heavily involved in the fighting from 1964 to 1973, though the US provided support both before and after this time frame.

This war has been called the "first television war," according to *Encyclopaedia Britannica*. For the first time in history, transportation and technology allowed news stories to be filmed on location, edited quickly, and shipped to the United States. There is debate about how much the media shaped public perception of the war. Some people think the news influenced people to hold certain beliefs. Others think the news reflected the public's viewpoint. Either way, media played a new role in this major world event.

Journalism shifted in a second way during the Vietnam War. Initially, reporters who were female were not allowed to stay overnight on the battlefield. This prevented them from doing their jobs. During the Vietnam War, the front line could move suddenly. If journalists traveled with troops, they could not guarantee they could be back to base before sunset. If a battle broke out after dark, the journalists could not leave the base. Reporters Anne Morrissy Merick and Ann Bryan Mariano organized the six other women who were stationed in Vietnam to cover the war. Merick and Mariano asked the US government to change the rule about women staying overnight. Their request was granted. Finally, women could report on the war just like men did.

A Golden Age of Investigative Journalism   **19**

Murrow's reporting led to the soldier's reinstatement. The next year, Murrow released an exposé of Senator Joseph McCarthy, who was leading the Red Scare. The US Senate conducted lengthy hearings at McCarthy's behest, much of which was broadcast on network news.

David Halberstam

All investigative journalists write articles challenging those who are in charge. The difference between their experiences often lies in how those people accept the exposure. Like President Teddy Roosevelt, leaders can rise to the challenge and make positive changes. Or they can be like President John F. Kennedy in response to David Halberstam's reporting from the Vietnam War. In October 1963, the president was so angry about the investigative journalist's reporting that he asked his employer, the New York Times, to transfer Halberstam out of Vietnam.

The Vietnam War is often mentioned, along with Watergate, as an event that allowed for the resurgence of investigative journalism. Despite the president's strongly worded request, the Times's publisher refused and even asked Halberstam to cancel his upcoming vacation so that it would be clear to everyone that he was not going anywhere. Halberstam would continue reporting on the war.

David Halberstam was born in 1934 in New York City and knew he wanted to be a journalist from a young age. He was managing editor of Harvard University's newspaper when he was a student there. After graduation, he wrote for newspapers in the South about the fledgling civil rights movement. The fight for racial equity affected the atmosphere in which journalists worked, allowing them to write more investigative pieces.

Soon after he arrived in Vietnam, in 1962, Halberstam realized he had doubts about US involvement and success in the war. His articles expressed this clearly. This led some to call him antiwar. According to William Prochnau, who wrote a book on Vietnam War reporting, Halberstam was not antiwar; instead, he was in favor of revealing military lies. The journalist "didn't say, 'You're not telling me the truth,'" Prochnau told the *New York Times*. "He said, 'You're lying.' He didn't mince words."

In 1964, Halberstam earned a Pulitzer Prize for his Vietnam reporting. According to the Brookings Institution, a public policy organization, Halberstam believed that "the job of the reporters in Vietnam was to report the news, whether or not the news was good for America."

Jessica Mitford

Investigative journalism was growing in popularity in the 1950s and 1960s, but that did not mean that newspapers and television studios were hiring lots of those reporters. It would always be risky to publish negative news about political and business leaders. The United States has freedom of the press. Still, powerful people can affect what stories are covered, when, and to what degree. Media outlets can be concerned that they may lose funding or good favor if they share negative stories about certain people. Jessica Mitford was one of the early midcentury investigative reporters who worked hard at her craft but could not find a regular employer. She was not on staff at any publication, so she instead worked as a freelancer.

Mitford was born in 1917 in England. Coming of age during Hitler's rise to power, Mitford solidified her political ideas at an early age. She knew her beliefs were far

22 *Watergate and Investigative Journalism*

Journalist Jessica Mitford was interviewed on the show *After Dark* in 1988. Mitford was a notable investigative journalist best known for her book *The American Way of Death*.

A Golden Age of Investigative Journalism

different from Hitler's, as well as from those of her parents and siblings, who sided with the Nazis. She moved to the United States in 1939. As a member of the Communist Party in the United States at a time when many people were scared of communism, Mitford found herself again tested in her beliefs.

Mitford became well known with her investigation of the American funeral industry. The *New York Times* called her 1963 book *The American Way of Death* a "classic of Muckraking journalism." She used her dark, biting humor to reveal that many people working in the funeral industry were charging too much for their services and products. Funerals are one of the most expensive purchases an American will make. Mitford learned from her husband's work with labor unions that union members' death benefits went almost entirely to pay for their funerals. Inspired by that tragic fact, she led her own investigation.

Nearly thirty years later, she revised the book that made her famous in investigative journalism. She added more negative details she had learned about the funeral industry. Her revision also predicted the rise of corporate funeral houses. Their business model increased profits for shareholders and increased costs for families. When Mitford died right before finishing her revision, she asked that the bill for her funeral be sent to Service Corporation International, one of the giants in the funeral industry. According to the *New York Times*, they never paid.

Getting Ready for the New Storytellers

The *Quill* cartoonists who expressed concern about television news also drew cartoons of hope for journalism in general. They believed that journalism was far from dead.

They knew they were entering a new era when journalism would be more important than ever.

In fact, they suggested with their drawings that sometimes there were too many stories to cover. In a June 1959 cartoon, a reporter says good-night to his boss as he leaves for the day. His boss, "Editor," is hidden behind stacks of paper. The viewer knows there is a person there only because of the column of dark smoke rising from a cigarette or maybe from a stressed-out mind.

In a December 1957 cartoon, a person labeled "Conscientious Reporter" kneels before a river made of "Propaganda," "Rumors," and "Sensationalism." He is panning for pieces of gold labeled "Facts." The cartoon is captioned "Tireless Prospector." This cartoon is saying that reporters are people who sift tirelessly through what is worthless to reveal something priceless.

The storytellers of Watergate stepped into that vital role.

Washington Post publisher Katharine Graham meets with managing editor Howard Simmons in 1973.

26 *Watergate and Investigative Journalism*

The Storytellers

Bob Woodward and Carl Bernstein are the two reporters often associated with Watergate and the investigative journalism boom of the early 1970s. Their work is among the most important, but they are not the only storytellers worth discussing. Their colleagues, sources, and publisher also made this story—and this new era of investigative journalism—happen.

Jack Anderson: Father of Modern Investigative Journalism

Jack Anderson was Woodward and Bernstein's predecessor as well as their contemporary. According to his *Washington Post* obituary in 2005, he was one of the few who could find mainstream work as an investigative reporter during the 1950s and 1960s. He "waged a one-man journalistic resistance when it was exceedingly unpopular to do so," his biographer, Mark Feldstein, told the *Post*. Within that

Journalist Jack Anderson lived from 1922 to 2005. He made his mark writing about wrongdoing, even though he knew powerful people would be angered by his articles.

28 *Watergate and Investigative Journalism*

wide-open space, Anderson made a name for himself. Because of Anderson's work, Woodward and Bernstein met with less resistance from the *Post* in the early 1970s. But Anderson saw there was still work to be done and was also still reporting in the 1970s. In fact, he won a Pulitzer Prize the very year Woodward and Bernstein exposed the Watergate scandal. (The trend of hard work would continue. Anderson refused to retire and worked almost up to his death.)

Jack Anderson was born in California in 1922 but was raised in Utah. He started working in media when he was twelve years old. His local newspaper, the *Deseret News*, published a regular feature on what was happening with the Boy Scouts, and Anderson edited that. Years later, when he was stationed with the merchant marines in China, he convinced the *Deseret News* to hire him as a foreign correspondent. The newspaper wanted him to write feel-good human-interest stories. Anderson found that boring. Instead, he sneaked onto a secret base operated by the Office of Strategic Services (OSS), which would become the Central Intelligence Agency (CIA). According to Anderson's *Washington Post* obituary, the OSS was not happy when they discovered he was there. However, they sent him on a lead to meet with Chinese nationalist guerrillas. No US newspaper was interested in what Anderson learned from the soldiers, that a civil war was happening in China. Later, he was drafted into the military, where Anderson continued to hone his reporting skills, working on military newspapers and for the Armed Forces Radio.

When Anderson left the military in 1947, he was ready to critically examine the system from the outside. He applied to work for Drew Pearson. Pearson had been exposing government corruption with his column Washington Merry-Go-Round since the 1930s. In 1969, Pearson died, and

Anderson took responsibility for the column. He stayed with it until 2001. At the height of its popularity, Washington Merry-Go-Round appeared in one thousand newspapers and was read daily by forty-five million people.

Anderson's *Washington Post* obituary quotes him as having once said, "I have to do daily what Woodward and Bernstein did once." He meant that Woodward and Bernstein made their names with one big news story: Watergate. Anderson, however, made a name for himself investigating numerous stories over about six decades, though none became as legendary as Watergate. Nonetheless, he had a lot of big scoops. From December 14, 1971, to January 20, 1972, he wrote about American policy decision-making during the Indo-Pakistan War. That earned him a Pulitzer Prize in 1972.

Anderson angered a lot of people with his work and his antics. People considered him "part circus huckster, part guerrilla fighter, part righteous rogue," Feldstein told the Post. He was not invited to the glitzy DC parties that other journalists attended. "The power elite saw him as an uncouth gossipmonger and shameless self-promoter," his *Washington Post* obituary says. The Nixon administration downright hated him. Nixon himself tried to smear Anderson's personal life. The CIA spied on him. An aide to the president ordered Anderson be poisoned.

Anderson was relentless in his pursuit of wrongdoers. He himself tried to live by an equally strict ethical code. Howard Kurtz, who worked for Anderson as one of his reporters and then as his ghostwriter, explained a rule he learned from the journalist: "When it came to the person under fire, Anderson said, 'Act like you're his defense lawyer.' In other words, make the strongest possible case for the innocence of the public figure you were prosecuting." Anderson wanted to reveal wrongdoing, but he wanted to do so fairly.

Bob Woodward

In 2014, four decades after Bob Woodward made his name as an investigative journalist on the Watergate story, he was still receiving praise for his work as an investigative reporter. That year, Robert Gates said he wished he had recruited the reporter into the Central Intelligence Agency (CIA) when he was the agency's director. Gates said, according to Woodward's website, that Woodward "has an extraordinary ability to get otherwise responsible adults to spill [their] guts to him … His ability to get people to talk about stuff they shouldn't be talking about is just extraordinary and may be unique." The fact that the United States' top spy organization wanted him to work for them indicates he was an excellent investigator, which is a huge part of being an outstanding investigative journalist.

Of course, writing effective articles is another huge part. Gene Roberts, former managing editor of the *New York Times*, says the Woodward and Bernstein coverage of Watergate was "maybe the single greatest reporting effort of all time." That is an impressive compliment, since the *Times* and the *Post* have been longtime competitors.

Bob Woodward was born in 1943 and grew up outside of Chicago. He studied history and English literature at Yale University. In 1970, he was a lieutenant in the US Navy. Sometimes he couriered documents between the military and the White House. One day, while he was sitting waiting for someone to receive his documents, he struck up a conversation with another man who was also waiting.

They spoke very casually at first. As Woodward recalled in a *Washington Post* article many years later, the other man did not seem to want to talk at all. Woodward, however, was desperate for conversation. "This was a time in my life of considerable anxiety, even consternation, about my future," he wrote. He was a new college graduate, and he had only one year left in his military service. He was taking graduate-level courses at George Washington University, but they were not pointing him in any direction. One class was in Shakespeare and the other was in international relations, two very different subjects. He had decided to talk to every interesting person he met, in hopes that they would inspire him in what to do next. Finally, Woodward learned the man's name, Mark Felt, and his job, assistant director of the Federal Bureau of Investigation (FBI). Specifically, Felt made sure that all FBI field offices were following procedures.

Woodward admitted later that he saw the conversation as a "career-counseling session." He asked the man for his phone number. Even though Felt had remained politely distant, he gave Woodward his contact information. The young man, only twenty-seven years old, used it. Woodward called Felt at work and at home. "I'm sure I poured out my heart," he wrote years later. From these conversations, Woodward decided not to go to law school, which he had been considering. This decision meant he had to figure out what to do after being discharged from the navy in August 1970.

He subscribed to the *Washington Post* and liked the "toughness and edge" he read in the news articles. On that alone, he decided to apply to be a reporter. Though Woodward had no experience, the paper decided to give him a two-week tryout. He failed at that major newspaper, but he loved the work. He took a job at a much smaller newspaper in Maryland. He also continued to develop his relationship with Felt and even had dinner at his house.

After a year spent learning the job of reporting, Woodward was offered another job at the *Post*. Not a year after that, he was breaking the biggest story of his career and one of the most important in US history. Felt turned from mentor and friend to inside source for Woodward's reporting on Watergate.

Since then, Woodward has written several books on US presidents as well as other leaders. He also still writes for the *Post*. In part because of Woodward's reporting, the *Post* won a Pulitzer Prize in 1973 for its Watergate coverage. In 2002, eleven *Post* articles on the 9/11 attacks won a Pulitzer; Woodward wrote seven of those. He has also won nearly every other major American award for journalism.

Carl Bernstein

Carl Bernstein was born in 1944 in Washington, DC. When he was only sixteen years old, he started working at a local paper, the *Washington Star*. He knew immediately that the newspaper life was the one for him. He was so convinced of this that he dropped out of the University of Maryland to work full-time at the *Star*. He had started as a copy boy, in many ways an errand runner around the newsroom. These were the days before email, so stories had to be physically carried around to different editors. He hoped to rise up the ranks and become a reporter.

Unfortunately, the *Star* would not let him be a reporter for them without a college degree. Similar to how Woodward would not give up, neither would his future

Woodward and Bernstein in 2017

Bob Woodward (*left*) and Carl Bernstein (*right*) attend the 2017 White House Correspondents' Association Dinner.

Once a storyteller, always a storyteller. Forty-five years after they broke the Watergate story, journalists Bob Woodward and Carl Bernstein were still talking about the changing shape of journalism and newsworthy events.

In November 2017, Woodward spoke about the state of journalism during the Trump administration. *USA Today*

Watergate and Investigative Journalism

reported Woodward as saying, "This is a test. Don't think this is just politics as usual, the way it's been with other presidents. This is different." Part of the difference, Woodward said, was that the public distrusted the media in 2017. There were stories for journalists to investigate, but the public may not be open to hearing them.

In October 2017, Bernstein spoke about the allegations that Russia was involved in the 2016 US presidential election. If that would turn out to be true, Bernstein said, it would be "worse than Watergate." The journalist said he saw parallels between the Russia allegations and Watergate. The *Chicago Tribune* reported him as saying, "If the allegations about Trump are true, that he colluded with Russia, then you have the president again willing to undermine the most basic part of our modern democratic system, which is free elections."

He also noted differences, saying, "We're a different country now—we're in a state of cold civil war in this country today and it didn't start with Donald Trump."

The Storytellers **35**

Washington Post Watergate colleague. Bernstein went to a newspaper that would accept him. He quickly proved himself, even winning an award from the New Jersey Press Association. He joined the *Washington Post* in 1966.

Though Bernstein left the newspaper ten years later, not long after breaking the Watergate story, he continued to work as an investigative journalist. He was on staff at ABC. He also wrote for major magazines like *Time* and *Rolling Stone*. As of 2017, he has written five books on world leaders and major historical events. He remains an important voice in political analysis, contributing to CNN and *Vanity Fair*.

Deep Throat

When it comes to investigative journalism, there can be no story without a source. Someone on the inside, who knows the secrets, must be willing to talk to the journalist trying to tell the story. In the case of Watergate, that source was known to the world for a long time as Deep Throat. In 2005, he chose to reveal his identity. His name is Mark Felt.

Felt was born in 1913 in Twin Falls, Idaho. He did well in his undergraduate work at the University of Idaho. He was even successful outside of the classroom; he was president of his fraternity. After graduating, he worked for Senator James P. Pope, a Democrat from Idaho, at his Washington, DC, office. At night, he took classes at George Washington University Law School.

The same year he passed the bar, the final test to become a lawyer, he started to train to become an FBI agent. During and immediately after World War II, Felt worked in the FBI's Espionage Section. He monitored the movement of Soviet spies. He also learned spying techniques from the Germans. This skill set would be useful decades later, when

Mark Felt appearing on *Face the Nation* in 1976

he sneaked information to Woodward and Bernstein about the Watergate scandal.

After college, Felt's career path progressed quickly. His work at the FBI did not change that. He received several promotions, including a major one in 1971. The FBI's director, J. Edgar Hoover, took notice of Felt's work and made him deputy associate director. This was the third-highest position in the FBI. When Hoover died, Felt became second in command. In this role, he led the FBI's investigation of the Watergate break-in.

No one, not even Woodward and Bernstein's fellow investigative journalists, knew how important Felt's information was to their work. Deep Throat's role was not detailed until the reporters' 1974 book *All the President's Men*. His real name was not revealed for another thirty years.

Felt retired from the FBI in 1973. He died in 2008, three and a half years after he told the world in a *Vanity Fair* article that he was Woodward and Bernstein's inside source.

Katharine Graham and the *Washington Post*

One element all storytellers must have is a place to tell their stories. Without such an outlet, those storytellers become just people with secrets. During Watergate, the *Washington Post* newspaper and its publisher, Katharine Graham, served that role for reporters Woodward and Bernstein.

Graham was born in 1917. Her family could have been the subject of a muckraker's pen. They were among the haves in a world of have-nots. One of Graham's best friends in school was President Ulysses S. Grant's granddaughter. Graham's mother was educated and also knew many of the famous people of the time, like philosopher John Dewey, painter Georgia O'Keefe, and sculptor Auguste Rodin. Graham's grandfather was a partner in an investment bank. Her father started his own investment firm and was soon a millionaire. He increased his fortune during World War I by starting a company to make dyes. The American textile industry had relied on dyes from Germany. During the war, Germany was an enemy of the United States, and there was no trade. Graham's father saved a lot of his money but also invested it. Along the way, he bought the *Washington Post*.

In addition to being wealthy and friendly with powerful people, Graham was smart. She attended Vassar College and

At the time of this photo, Katharine Graham was president of the Washington Post Company.

The Storytellers

then the University of Chicago. The university attracted lots of radical, left-thinking students; some were even communists. Graham kept telling them that she could not argue with a capitalist system that had treated her family so well.

In 1940, she married, and her husband eventually became the publisher of the *Post*. For the next twenty-three years, Graham raised their four children. Then, when she was only forty-six years old, her husband died. Suddenly, in 1963, Graham found herself in an unexpected role. She was the *Post*'s publisher. She was one of the first women to be a major business leader in the United States. According to her obituary in the *Economist* magazine, Graham had a favorite story of her own that she liked to tell. She visited a village in the African country of Côte d'Ivoire. The town's chief welcomed her by saying he was honored to be visited by the seventeenth most important person in the world. Graham thought this was funny, perhaps because it was so specific.

Despite being a powerful woman, Graham did not consider herself a feminist. Gloria Steinem, one of the most famous feminists of the time (and still today), could not even convince her. Graham's incredible wealth probably influenced her thinking. She called herself a "limousine liberal." In her 1997 autobiography, she reflected on her perspective leading up to the 1970s. She claimed to believe in progressive ideals, but her privilege may have prevented her from fully understanding how policy affected people. Over time, a new female friend, who was also one of Graham's newspaper editors, helped her to understand. "Though it took me a long time to throw off my early and ingrained assumptions," Graham wrote in her autobiography, "I did come to understand the importance of the basic problems of equality in the workplace, upward mobility, salary equity, and, more recently, child care."

She tried to be friendly with President Nixon, but that relationship was doomed. In 1971, she approved the *Washington Post*'s publishing of the Pentagon Papers. These were once-secret government documents about the Vietnam War. The Nixon administration took legal action against the newspaper. During Watergate, the Washington Post Company was in danger of losing its television affiliates, but Graham stood by her investigative team, which pitted her against the country's president.

These experiences did not drive Graham away from conservative politics. She became friends with Henry Kissinger and his wife, as well as President Ronald and First Lady Nancy Reagan. According to her *Guardian* obituary, Graham was shaken by her confrontation with the press workers' union in 1975. For more than four months, the people who ran the *Washington Post*'s presses, which printed the newspaper, engaged in a sometimes violent strike. Machines were damaged, and people were hurt. Graham herself was a target of the workers' anger. They were not just angry at their working conditions or at management in general but at her. That sent her allegiance perhaps somewhat away from progressives and toward conservatives.

The Almost-Storytellers

Woodward, Bernstein, the *Washington Post*, and Deep Throat are known as Watergate's main storytellers. Deep Throat provided the inside information that journalists Woodward and Bernstein needed to unravel the mystery. Because of the newspaper's encouragement, the two reporters could spend months on one story. When an article was ready, the *Post* was there to publish it.

L. Patrick Gray testifies before the Senate Watergate Committee in 1973.

However, there was a moment when those four almost didn't become Watergate's storytellers. If events had twisted a slightly different direction, we would have known the names Smith, Phelps, and L. Patrick Gray in connection with Watergate instead. In 2009, thirty-seven years after Watergate, two people, Robert Smith and Robert Phelps, revealed that they almost broke the story before Woodward and Bernstein did. Smith had been a reporter for the *New York Times*, and Phelps had been an editor there.

Two months after the Watergate burglary, Smith had lunch with the acting director of the Federal Bureau of Investigation (FBI), L. Patrick Gray. It was August 16, 1972, and the next day, Smith was scheduled to leave town to attend Yale Law School. He had already quit his job as a *Times* reporter. Throughout his work with the newspaper, Smith had developed a good relationship with Gray. The lunch was meant as a friendly good-bye. Gray's son later explained to the *New York Times* that the lunch "was more between a mentor and a young man than between an acting director of the F.B.I. and a reporter."

So when the topic of Watergate came up in their conversation, Gray "let his hair down a little bit," his son explained. Gray shared secrets about the case with Smith. Gray's son said he did this because he was just having a casual conversation. Gray "didn't think [Smith] was a reporter anymore."

Smith was not employed as a reporter, but that did not mean he had lost his journalistic instinct. Smith told the *New York Times* in 2009 that he was stunned as Gray talked that summer day in 1972. "He told me the attorney general was involved in a cover-up," Smith told the newspaper, "and I said, 'How high does it go? To the president?' And he sat

All the President's Men: A Unique Movie About a Unique Time

The storytelling about Watergate has lasted much longer than the actual scandal. Woodward and Bernstein's book about their investigation, *All the President's Men*, became the fastest-selling nonfiction hardcover in the United States when it was published three months before President Nixon resigned. Two years later, in 1976, screenwriter William Goldman and director Alan J. Pakula brought the story to the big screen. Only four other movies that year made more money than their movie adaptation, which was also called *All the President's Men*.

The movie's success was surprising. This was a story about a recent event, so the public could have been tired of hearing about it. Also, the audience already knew how the story ended. Plus, the main action was mostly the two heroes reading documents, typing, and talking with people—not exactly thrilling stuff for viewers.

According to an essay about the movie by reporter and critic Mark Feeney, "What's so charismatic about journalism here isn't its practitioners … it's the idea of journalism." An example of this is the movie's famous opening scene. It is such a tight close-up on a blindingly white piece of paper that the viewer doesn't even know it's a piece of paper—until a typewriter key strikes, printing a letter but sounding like gunfire.

Feeney explains the purpose of making typing look so dramatic: "What we will see for the next two hours and 19

Actors Dustin Hoffman (*left*) and Robert Redford (*right*) portrayed Carl Bernstein and Bob Woodward in *All the President's Men*.

minutes is a display of the power of the word and, something utterly new to the newspaper movie genre, the *purity* of the word." Indeed, the story about Watergate is more than a story about political scandal. It's also a story about storytelling.

The Storytellers 45

there and looked at me and he didn't answer. His answer was in the look."

After lunch, Smith went straight back to the *Times*'s Washington, DC, office. He was "in a super-charged state," he remembered. He found Phelps. "I was too excited to sit down," Smith said. "I paced up and back." While he paced, he told the newspaper editor what Gray had said. Phelps recorded the conversation and took notes. In hindsight, we know they had one of the biggest stories of the century literally in black and white in front of them. In that moment, however, life was already moving on past Watergate.

Smith had a schedule to keep and did indeed leave the city the next day. Phelps was preparing for a monthlong trip to Alaska. The newspaper staff in general was completely focused on the Republican National Convention, which was starting on August 21. The country would be voting for a president that November. A presidential election was always a big story.

In fact, Phelps admitted years later to the *Times*, he quickly forgot all about that talk with Smith. When he started to write his memoir nearly forty years later, Smith reminded him of it. By that time, Phelps could not remember what he had done with the tape or his notes from the conversation. He also could not remember if he had told any of his colleagues about the information from Gray. And he could not remember the answer to the biggest question of all: "We never developed Gray's tips into publishable stories," Phelps wrote in his memoir. "Why we failed is a mystery to me."

Seymour Hersh

Seymour Hersh has been working as an investigative journalist for decades. He is perhaps the third best-known

Journalist Seymour Hersh won a Pulitzer Prize in 1970.

newspaper reporter connected to the Watergate story. After a few months of Woodward and Bernstein's coverage for the *Washington Post*, Hersh started writing about it for the *Post*'s competitor, the *New York Times*. Yet even the *Post* would acknowledge in a 2015 article, "Although Woodward and Carl Bernstein are the journalists most closely associated with the Watergate scandal, Hersh played an important role." Hersh is known for having a personality that is the opposite of Woodward's. Mark Plotkin, a political columnist and pundit who knows Hersh, wondered to the *Washington Post* about the man. "How does he get people to tell him things? He's not a seducer," but he manages to convince people "to reveal things that are deeply secretive." Plotkin suggested that maybe where others use charm to encourage people to confide in them, Hersh uses his "South Side, belligerent, Chicago, in-your-face" personality to knock people off their guard.

    Seymour Hersh was born in 1937 on the South Side of Chicago, only a few miles from where Woodward would be born six years later. He had a twin brother. Their father had immigrated from Lithuania, their mother from Poland. Hersh has said they were apolitical, not really involved in politics, because they were too busy working.

    He did not do well in high school, so he enrolled in community college. Only a few days into his college career, one of his teachers recognized his natural intellect. He took Hersh to the University of Chicago and got him enrolled.

    After graduation, Hersh studied law for a year and then started working in newspapers. He worked his way up in the Associated Press and became known as the figurehead of the next generation of muckrakers. "I wasn't editor of the Yale *Daily News*, or the Harvard *Crimson*," Hersh told the *Guardian*, "and 11 years after getting into college, I'm sticking two fingers into the eye of a Republican president, getting prizes and enough money to buy my first house. I mean, it's a pretty amazing society we live in."

The People Who Chased the Scoop

When it comes to the investigative journalism of Watergate, the storytellers are a varied group. There are, of course, the journalists whose names left a deep impression on the public, like Bob Woodward, Carl Bernstein, and Seymour Hersh. There are also the many, like Jack Anderson, whose work is less known but no less important. Investigative stories are the type that are scooped—not everyone can get the first big byline on a story that will make one big first impression. So people like Robert Smith and Robert Phelps are also part of the storytellers, even though many no longer recognize their names. Finally, investigative journalists rely on media to get their stories to the public. Fearless leaders such as Katharine Graham and her *Washington Post* don't write the stories, but they are as much the tellers of them as those who do.

The Weather

Today—Rain, high in the low to mid 70s, low in the mid to upper 60s. Chance of rain is 60 per cent today, 0 per cent tonight. Saturday — Cloudy, high around 80. Yesterday's temp. range, 77-68. Details, Page D19.

The Washington Post

FINA[L]

112 Pages — 4 S[ections]

Amusements D 1 Me[tro] | Classified C14 Obi[tuaries] | Comics D20 Out | Editorials A30 Spo[rts] | Fed. Diary D21 Sty[le] | Financial C 9 TV

97th Year .... No. 247 © 1974, The Washington Post Co. FRIDAY, AUGUST 9, 1974 Phone (202) 223-6000 Classified 223-6200 Circulation 223-6100 20c Beyond Washington, Maryland and Virginia

Nixon Resigns

By Carroll Kilpatrick
Washington Post Staff Writer

Richard Milhous Nixon announced last night that he will resign as the 37th President of the United States at noon today.

Vice President Gerald R. Ford of Michigan will take the oath as the new President at noon to complete the remaining 2½ years of Mr. Nixon's term.

After two years of bitter public debate over the Watergate scandals, President Nixon bowed to pressures from the public and leaders of his party to become the first President in American history to resign.

"By taking this action," he said in a subdued yet dramatic television address from the Oval Office, "I hope that I will have hastened the start of the process of healing which is so desperately needed in America."

Vice President Ford, who spoke a short time later in front of his Alexandria home, announced that Secretary of State Henry A. Kissinger will remain in his Cabinet.

The President-to-be praised Mr. Nixon's sacrifice for the country and called it "one of the very saddest incidents that I've ever witnessed."

Mr. Nixon said he decided he must resign when he concluded that he no longer had "a strong enough political base in the Congress" to make it possible for him to complete his term of office.

Declaring that he has never been a quitter, Mr. Nixon said that to leave office before the end of his term "is abhorrent to every instinct in my body."

But "as President, I must put the interests of America first," he said.

While the President acknowledged that some of his judgments "were wrong," he made no confession of the "high crimes and misdemeanors" with which the House Judiciary Committee charged him in its bill of impeachment.

Specifically, he did not refer to Judiciary Committee charges that in the cover-up of Watergate crimes he misused government agencies such as the FBI, the Central Intelligence Agency and the Internal Revenue Service.

After the President's address, Special Prosecutor Leon Jaworski issued a statement declaring that "there has been no agreement or understanding of any sort between the President or his representatives and the special prosecutor relating in any way to the President's resignation."

Jaworski said that his office "was not asked for any such agreement or understanding and offered none."

His office was informed yesterday afternoon of the President's decision, Jaworski said, but "my office did not participate in any way in the President's decision to resign."

Mr. Nixon's brief speech was delivered in firm tones and he appeared to be in complete control of hi[s] ... The absence of rancor contrasted sharply wit[h] ... well" he delivered in 1962 after being defea[ted for] governorship of California.

An hour before the speech, however, th[e] ... broke down during a meeting with old c[ongressional] friends and had to leave the room.

He had invited 20 senators and 26 represe[ntatives to] a farewell meeting in the Cabinet room. Later ... M. Goldwater (R-Ariz.), one of those prese[nt] ... Nixon said to them very much what he said in ...

"He just told us that the country couldn't ... a half-time President," Goldwater reported. ... broke down and cried and he had to leave ... Then the rest of us broke down and cried."

In his televised resignation, after thanking ... for their support, the President concluded b[y] ... was leaving office "with this prayer: may Go[d be] with you in all the days ahead."

As for his sharpest critics, the President s[aid] ... with no bitterness toward those who have o[pposed] ... He called on all Americans to "join togeth[er] ... helping our new President succeed."

The President said he had thought it was ... persevere in office in face of the Watergate ... to complete his term.

"In the past days, however, it has become ... me that I no longer have a strong enough p[olitical base] in the Congress to justify continuing that ... Nixon said.

His family "unanimously urged" him to s[tay] and fight the charges against him, he said. ... to realize that he would not have the suppo[rt] ... carry out the duties of his office in difficult ...

"America needs a full-time President and ... Congress," Mr. Nixon said. The resignation ... "a great sadness that I will not be here in ... to complete work on the programs started, ...

But praising Vice President Ford, Mr. Nix[on said] "the leadership of America will be in good h[ands]."

In his admission of error, the outgoing Pr[esident said] "I deeply regret any injuries that may have ... the course of the events that led to this deci[sion]."

He emphasized that world peace had bee[n the] riding concern of his years in the White ...

When he first took the oath, he said, he ma[de a] commitment" to "consecrate my office and ... the cause of peace among nations."

"I have done my very best in all the days ... true to that pledge," he said, adding that ... confident that the world is a safer place fo[r] ...

"This more than anything is what I hope[d] ... when I sought the presidency." Mr. Nixon ... more than anything is what I hope will be ... you, to our country, as I leave the preside[ncy]."

Noting that he had lived through a turb[ulent] ... he recalled a statement of Theodore Roosev[elt] ... man "in the arena whose face is marred ... sweat and blood" and who, if he fails "a[t least fails] while daring greatly."

Mr. Nixon placed great emphasis on his ... foreign affairs. He said his administration ha[d opened] the doors that for a quarter of a century st[ood] ... the United States and the People's Republic ...

In the Mideast, he said, the United States ... to build on the peace in that area. And wit[h the Soviet] Union, he said, the administration had begun ... of ending the nuclear arms race. The goal ... is to reduce and finally destroy those arms ... threat of nuclear war will no longer ha[ng over the] world." The two countries, he added, "must ... in cooperation rather than in confrontation."

Mr. Nixon has served 2,026 days as the 3[7th President] of the United States. He leaves office with 2½ ... second term remaining to be carried out by ... nominated to be Vice President last year.

Yesterday morning, the President confer[red with his] successor. He spent much of the day in h[is Executive] Office Building hideaway working on his ... attending to last-minute business.

At 7:30 p.m., Mr. Nixon again left the Whi[te House for] the short walk to the Executive Office Bu[ilding. A] crowd outside the gates waved U.S. flags and ... ica" as he walked slowly up the steps, his ... alone.

At the EOB, Mr. Nixon met for a little ove[r] ... with the leaders of Congress—James O. Eastla[nd] ... president pro tem to the Senate; Mike Mansfi[eld] ... Senate majority leader; Hugh Scott (R-Pa.), S[enate] ...

See RESIGN, A7, Col. 1

Ford Assumes Presidency Today

By Jules Witcover
Washington Post Staff Writer

Gerald Rudolph Ford Jr., a Grand Rapids, Mich., lawyer [w]ho never aspired to national office but had it thrust upon [h]im as a result of two of the greatest political scandals [i]n American history, will become the 38th President of the [U]nited States at noon today.

He will be the first American President not elected to [n]ational office by the people, having been nominated Vice [P]resident by President Nixon last Oct. 12 under provi[si]ons of the new 25th Amendment to the Constitution.

Last night, immediately after watching Mr. Nixon's tele[vi]sed announcement that he is resigning, Ford walked [o]nto the lawn of his Alexandria home, praised the Presi[de]nt for deciding to step aside and pledged to continue [M]r. Nixon's foreign policy "that has achieved peace and [b]uilt the future blocks for peace."

Ford announced that he had asked Secretary of State [H]enry A. Kissinger, whom he called "a very great man," [to] stay on in the new administration and that Kissinger [ha]d accepted. "He and I will be working together in the [pu]rsuit of peace in the future, as we have achieved it in [th]e past," he said.

Ford is expected to keep on and have the support of [th]e entire Nixon Cabinet, which promises to give him [a]n initial period of stability. But even before he is sworn [in], he faces some squabbling within his own party over [th]e question of the Vice President he will choose. Some [co]nservatives were openly advocating yesterday that for[m]er New York Gov. Nelson A. Rockefeller be dropped [fr]om consideration.

Ford, speaking calmly before a battery of microphones [an]d under hot TV lights in the summer night, also pledged [to] address himself to domestic problems by working in a [s]pirit of cooperation" with Congress, where he served [in] the House for 25 years.

"I've been very fortunate in my lifetime in public office [to] have a good many adversaries in the political arena in [Co]ngress," he said, "but I don't think I have a single [en]emy in the Congress. And the net result is that I think [to]morrow I can start out working with Democrats and [Re]publicans, in the House as well as in the Senate, to [wo]rk on the problems, serious ones, which we have at [ho]me."

The Vice President called the turn of events that has [br]ought him to the presidency "one of the most difficult [an]d very saddest periods, and one of the very saddest [in]cidents, that I've ever witnessed."

He said President Nixon "has made one of the greatest [pe]rsonal sacrifices for the country, and one of the finest [pe]rsonal decisions on behalf of all of us as Americans, [by] his decision to resign as President of the United [St]ates."

"I pledge to you tonight," he concluded, "as I will [pl]edge tomorrow and in the future, my best efforts and [co]operation and leadership and dedication to do what's [go]od for America and good for the world."

The swearing in of the new President is to take place [at] noon at the White House. The ceremony will be held [in] the Rose Garden if the weather is good, and in the [Ea]st Room if it is not. The U.S. Weather Service said [las]t night there was a 60 per cent chance of rain today. [F]ord is to speak briefly to the nationwide television [au]dience after being sworn in, and according to congres-

See FORD, A12, Col. 1

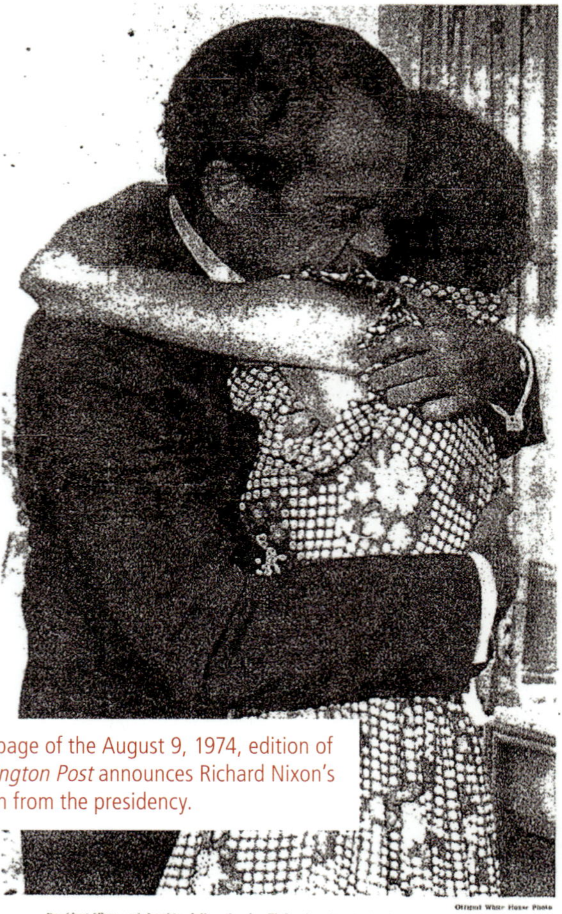

Official White House Photo

President Nixon and daughter Julie embracing Wednesday after the President's decision to resign.

The Washington Post THE NIXON YEARS

A 24-page special section on the Nixon presidency—inside today.

[E]ra of Good Feeling

Congress Expects H...

By Spencer Rich and Richard ...
Washington Post Staff Writers

[F]rom one end of Capitol ... to the other, members [of] Congress predicted last [nigh]t that the presidency of [Ger]ald R. Ford will start [with] a new era of good feel[ing] between Congress and [the] White House, helping to ... the deep and wrenching ... the nation's govern[me]nt has suffered in the ... two years.

[T]he tone was set by the ... moeratic leaders of the [Hou]se and the Senate, both [of] whom have served with ... on terms of close co[op]eration during his 25 years [in] Congress before he be[cam]e Vice President.

[G]erry Ford is a personal [frie]nd," said House Speaker [Carl] Albert (D-Okla.). "I am ... our relationship will be ...

[S]enate Majority Leader [Mik]e Mansfield (D-Mont.) ... "He's a decent man, ... conservative but you know wh... give con... gressiona... get excep...

The pr... to Presid... tion was ... that Congress and the nation have been spared the agony of a House vote and Senate trial that would force each member to be counted and divide the nation.

House leaders of both parties said the tone of the President's resignation speech satisfied them and they didn't see any need to go ahead with a floor vote on impeachment. Albert said, "The manner of his leaving was, I think, one of his best efforts. I believe that bitterness was averted by the tone of his speech ... he went out not trying to say he was framed."

See CONGRESS, A9, Col. 1

A Solemn Cha[nge]

Power Is Passed Quie[tly]

By Richard Harwood and Haynes Joh[nson]
Washington Post Staff Writers

When the day finally came, the anger and tensions and recriminations that had so enveloped this capital for weeks had been subdued in the solemnity of change. A sense of calm and a tenuous spirit of conciliation began to emerge.

There was no chorus of jubilation in Washington and no cries for vengeance or retribution. There was an absence of turmoil, mobs, violence, massive protests.

The crowds that began gathering at the White House on Tuesday remained quiet, solemn and patient. They were witnesses to history, yes, and someday they would tell their grandchildren about it. But now on this Thursday, Aug. 8, 1974, they seemed more preoccupied by personal feelings of sorrow and sadness.

"Think of it, ... ist from Whe... most beautiful ... the country, ri... street, and th... lives there. Th... all his life to ... to give it up. ... terrible thing, h... it all on him ... makes me sad ... be humiliated ..."

Another vis... driven up ... Beach, S.C., w... cal: "Our cou... vive. In a wa... the Kennedy ... It is a sad tim... but we'll pull ..."

"By nightfal... had swelled to ... tions, blocking ... toric Pennsylv... filling up beau... Park with its ... benches and s...

See DAY, ...

The front page of the August 9, 1974, edition of the *Washington Post* announces Richard Nixon's resignation from the presidency.

3

Watergate's Stories

The stories of the Watergate era are vast. As always, the world was experiencing things like war and corruption, but the news coverage of these events was stronger than ever. This chapter focuses on the Watergate scandal itself as a crucial example of investigative journalism. It does not ignore an example of major reporting from Vietnam, however. In the reporting on both Vietnam and Watergate, we can see the same authors and investigative techniques.

The My Lai Massacre and Cover-Up

Seymour Hersh won a Pulitzer Prize in 1970 for his reporting of the 1968 My Lai Massacre, during which US soldiers killed hundreds of unarmed residents of My Lai and set fire to the South Vietnamese village. His reporting was incredibly important because it revealed a US government cover-up of the massacre. Yet Hersh's effect on journalism was also important. His work created demand for more investigative reporting. Just a few years later, Woodward and Bernstein would meet that demand with their stories on Watergate.

Hersh explained the context of his My Lai reporting to radio program *Democracy Now!* on the fiftieth anniversary of the massacre. Richard Nixon had defeated Hubert Humphrey for the US presidency with the promise that he would end the Vietnam War. In truth, Nixon's plan was to win it, Hersh said, "and so, antiwar feelings were getting high." Both civilians and members of the military were upset. Hersh recalled a lot of desertions. Soldiers abandoned their posts because they disagreed so strongly with their orders. He followed the story of a hearing in Detroit, Michigan, that relied on the testimony of several GIs speaking out against the US military. Hersh guessed that for every story that made the news, there were many more that had not. "I knew how much there was an underbelly of very ugly stuff in that war that wasn't being reported," he told *Democracy Now!*

One day, a lawyer involved in antiwar issues gave Hersh a tip about My Lai. He said that a soldier at Fort Benning, an army base in Georgia, was being charged with murdering at least 109 Vietnamese civilians. Hersh was interested. He was a freelance journalist, so he was always on the hunt for a story. As he did not have an editor to assign him stories, he had to find his own.

Hersh immediately went to work investigating. He ran into a colonel he knew at the Pentagon. Hersh had served in the military, so he relied on his knowledge of how to talk with soldiers. He teased the colonel about his limp because, he said, that kind of mean humor is very common in the military. He was right about his technique. The colonel talked. He said enough so that Hersh knew he had a story.

According to the *Guardian*, Hersh then knocked on doors at Fort Benning until he found the soldier accused of the

American soldiers set fire to homes in My Lai, South Vietnam, in 1968.

murders. Again calling on his skill connecting with soldiers, Hersh bought the man steaks and bourbon and made him comfortable by going to the soldier's girlfriend's home. Hersh was "naturally appalled" about what the soldier had done. However, the *Guardian* wrote, "his first thought … was 'Pulitzer prize. My career's made if I do this right.'"

For weeks, no newspaper would buy his story. Finally, Hersh brought his articles to Dispatch News Service. The antiwar news agency got the story placed. Eventually, thirty-six newspapers ran his story. Hersh told *Democracy Now!*, "The American press, they may not be aggressive, but if you do stuff that they think is right, they will publish it."

Many people did not like that he told this story. Hersh told the *Guardian* he was "scared" for his safety. Still, he kept reporting as the story unfolded.

Political Cartoonists of the Watergate Era

In 1997, political cartoonists celebrated the twenty-fifth anniversary of Woodward and Bernstein breaking the news about the Watergate scandal. Reporters worked hard on that story. So, too, did cartoonists. Paul Conrad, with the *Los Angeles Times*, and Doug Marlette, with *Newsday*, spoke on a panel about cartooning during Watergate. Moderator Sandy Northop, who wrote a history of political cartooning, said, "Watergate was the second golden age of American political cartooning."

She suggested that the first time political cartooning held an important role in American media was one hundred years before Watergate. The "father of political cartooning," Thomas Nast, used his cartoons to relentlessly attack the corrupt New York politician Boss Tweed. Tweed remained the symbol of political evil until President Nixon. Then, cartoonists presented a new image of political wrongdoing to the public.

Marlette agreed. He said the entire era provided great training for political cartoonists. There was the war abroad and the civil rights movement at home. Watergate, he said, "topped it off." He quipped, "Bad times for the republic are good times for satire."

In contrast, Marlette felt that the passion had gone out of cartooning by the late 1990s. Political cartoons always reflect

This 1973 political cartoon by Jean-Claude Suares shows how audio tapes could destroy the White House during the Watergate investigation.

the times, he said. So, "in the kind of squishy [President Bill] Clinton years, you get kind of squishy cartoons." Marlette said that in the late 1960s, he used cartooning to prove he was a conscientious objector. This meant he was against the Vietnam War and would not fight in it. In other words, he was making cartoons powerful enough to prove his political convictions.

Watergate Itself

Watergate began with a burglary and ended with the resignation of a US president. Throughout it all, the press was there, investigating. From the beginning, the *Washington Post* was on the Watergate case. First, we'll look at a short version of the Watergate timeline. Then, we'll learn about Woodward's and Bernstein's experiences investigating.

Timeline of a Story

Alfred E. Lewis was the first reporter to file a story on Watergate on June 18, 1972. He wrote that five men, one of whom used to work for the CIA, were arrested in the Watergate residential and office complex in Washington, DC. They seemed to be trying to bug the offices of the Democratic National Committee (DNC). They were carrying listening devices, lockpicks, cash, photography equipment, a shortwave receiver that could pick up police radio calls, and tear gas guns. Two filing cabinet drawers were open. The burglars might have been interrupted while they were taking photos of confidential documents. Two ceiling panels from the office of a Democratic Party secretary had been removed. "Her office is adjacent to the office of Democratic National Chairman Lawrence F. O'Brien," Lewis said. "Presumably, it would have been possible to

The media interviews Frank Wills, the security guard on duty during the Watergate break-in.

slide a bugging device through the panels in that office to a place above the ceiling panels in O'Brien's office."

With the next article, on June 19, Woodward and Bernstein began their reporting. They uncovered that one of the burglars, the former CIA employee, provided security for

Watergate's Stories **57**

Woodward, Bernstein, and the Demand for Information

According to Bob Woodward and Carl Bernstein, they were able to crack the Watergate case because technology was not a factor in 1972 the way it is in the twenty-first century.

In 2012, they spoke at the American Society of News Editors' annual conference. The speech was covered by *Techpresident*. The veteran reporters told the editors about an experience they had speaking recently with undergraduate journalism students. The students said that if Watergate happened in the twenty-first century, they would solve it in a few short days. They reasoned that they could search for clues and answers on the internet.

The students thought the internet "was a magic lantern that lit up all events," Woodward said at the conference. Trusting so fully in the internet is dangerous, according to the veteran reporters. "The truth of what goes on is not on the internet," Woodward said. "The truth resides with people. Human sources."

Woodward talked to the students' professor. He said, "Your students have a heart-stopping over-confidence in the quality of the information on the internet." To the *Techpresident* reporter, he added, "There's nothing laughable about this. It's sad."

The *Techpresident* reporter explored further. "Trying to imagine how Watergate would have played out in the age of the internet is to some degree impossible," he wrote, "because the internet is also a product of Watergate."

The next generation of journalists work together on a story.

The internet has in part become so popular because the average person demands access to lots of information. And they demand this in part because people like Woodward and Bernstein exposed a level of truth we had never seen before. Journalism students today, he wrote, "owe Woodward, Bernstein and the other reporters who broke Watergate open a huge debt for making that so."

Watergate's Stories **59**

the Republican National Committee (RNC). John N. Mitchell, formerly the US attorney general and then the leader of the Committee for the Reelection of the President, Richard Nixon's campaign organization, said the burglars "were not operating either in our behalf or with our consent."

In their September 29 article, Woodward and Bernstein reported that John Mitchell, while serving as attorney general, had "personally controlled a secret Republican fund that was used to gather information about the Democrats."

By mid-fall, Woodward and Bernstein were reporting that the FBI had connected the Watergate burglary with the White House. They wrote on October 10, "The Watergate bugging incident stemmed from a massive campaign of political spying and sabotage conducted on behalf of President Nixon's re-election and directed by officials of the White House and the Committee for the Re-election of the President."

With the new year, there was clearly a Watergate "beat," and Woodward and Bernstein led it. However, they also had help from other reporters. Lawrence Meyer's article on January 31, 1973, reported about major convictions of people close to the president. G. Gordon Liddy and James W. McCord Jr. were convicted of conspiracy, burglary, and wiretapping. They were former aides to Nixon. Another former White House aide decided not to wait for a conviction. E. Howard Hunt, also a CIA agent, pleaded guilty to the charges against him. "Two days after the break-in White House consultant Hunt was linked to the five suspects," Meyer wrote.

Opposite: President Richard Nixon says he is "not a crook" at a press conference on November 17, 1973.

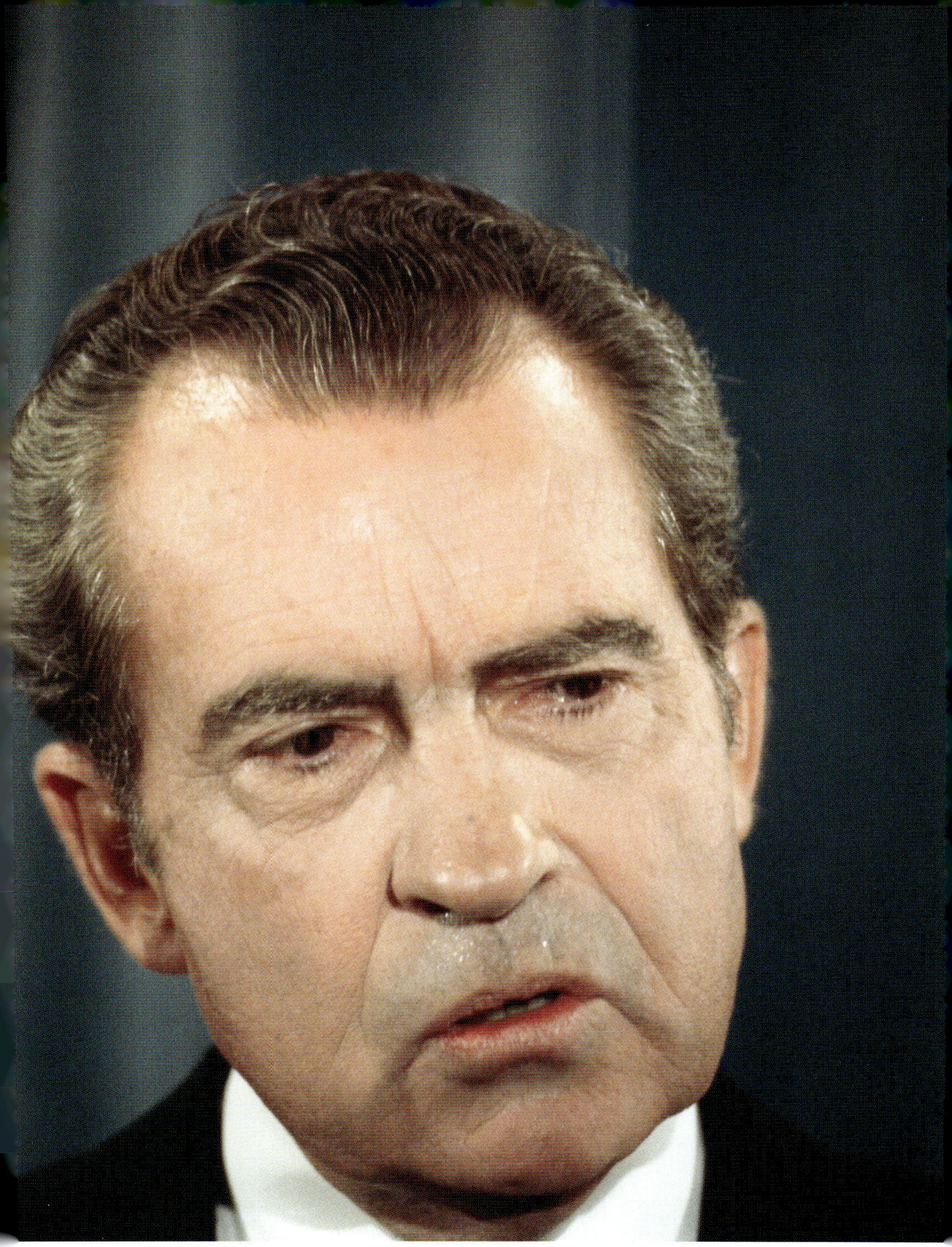

Woodward and Bernstein brought the president into the picture in their June 3, 1973, article for the *Post*. John Dean, who had at one time been one of the president's lawyers, told investigators that he "discussed aspects of the Watergate cover-up with President Nixon or in Mr. Nixon's presence on at least 35 occasions."

The investigative journalists learned about evidence that may prove these conversations existed. On July 17, Meyer reported that President Nixon had been recording conversations that happened in the White House. He used "several hidden recording devices." This was important because the tapes could prove when the president first learned about the Watergate cover-up. On July 24, Carroll Kilpatrick's *Washington Post* story reported that President Nixon refused to release the tapes of those recorded conversations to investigators. By doing this, he "set the stage ... for a major constitutional confrontation."

President Nixon addressed the public on November 17. Kilpatrick reported that the president held a televised meeting with four hundred managing editors from the Associated Press. He told them, "People have got to know whether or not their President is a crook. Well, I'm not crook."

The Senate already had some of the taped White House conversations in their possession, as of October 23. On November 22, *Washington Post* reporter George Lardner Jr. reported on these tapes. There was an eighteen-and-a-half-minute gap in one of the tapes. That gap happened to come in a conversation that took place on June 20, three days after the Watergate break-in. According to Archibald Cox the former special prosecutor in the Watergate case, "there is every reason to infer that the meeting included discussion of the Watergate incident."

Richard Nixon leaves the White House after resigning from the presidency.

The next nine months were intense—for the politicians involved in the story, the investigative journalists covering it, and the public opening their newspapers to new information every day. On August 9, 1974, Richard Nixon became the first US president to resign. He announced his intention on August 8. *Washington Post* reporter Kilpatrick reported on it the following day. "While the President acknowledged that some of his judgments 'were wrong,'" Kilpatrick wrote, "he made no confession of the 'high crimes and misdemeanors' with which the House Judiciary Committee charged him in its

Watergate's Stories **63**

bill of impeachment." (The Judiciary Committee had passed three articles of impeachment between July 27 and July 30, 1974. Next, the matter would have gone to the whole House—but Nixon resigned before that could happen.)

The president said that, after two years, the situation had gone on too long. He said he hated to quit, but he worried about "the interests of America." He also said that he no longer had "a strong enough political base in the Congress." As part of his job to investigate the full story, Kilpatrick interviewed the people closest to the president. Senator Barry M. Goldwater, a Republican from Arizona, was one of the twenty US senators and twenty-six US representatives whom Nixon invited to a farewell meeting an hour before he gave his resignation speech. Goldwater told Kilpatrick that Nixon said to the group of friends and colleagues gathered there "that the country couldn't operate with a half-time President. Then he broke down and cried and he had to leave the room. Then the rest of us broke down and cried."

Interestingly, Woodward and Bernstein never interviewed Nixon during their writing of the Watergate story. Both told NPR, on the fortieth anniversary of the scandal, that they would have asked Nixon, "Why?" Why would he go to such risky extremes? "Why" is a simple but effective question that all investigative journalists use. They are always trying to learn the truth behind the situation.

The Journey of Two Investigative Journalists

At 8:30 a.m. on June 17, 1972, a phone call at home woke Woodward. His editor at the *Washington Post* was asking him to come in to cover a burglary that seemed strange.

By the next day, Woodward was reporting that five men, including one former employee of the CIA, had broken into the DNC offices to bug them.

Part of the Job Is Getting Hung Up On

By the second day after the break-in, Bernstein was working with Woodward. Together, they connected one of the burglars to the RNC. They also guessed that they could connect the burglars to E. Howard Hunt. In one of the burglars' address books, they had found his phone number along with the notes "W. House" and "W.H.," meaning "White House."

Woodward called Felt for information and guidance. As he said in a piece he wrote for the *Washington Post* years later, "This was the moment when a source or friend in the investigative agencies of government is invaluable." Felt said he did not want to talk at the office, but he also did not ignore Woodward's request for information about Watergate. He said the burglary case would soon "heat up." Then he hung up.

Woodward was intrigued. He also could not wait for Felt to leave the office for the day and maybe take a second call from Woodward. He had a deadline—he was supposed to produce another article on the burglary for the next day's paper.

So, Woodward decided to try to reach Hunt on his own. He simply called the White House and asked to speak with him. The operator suggested he might be in the office of Nixon's special counsel. (A special counsel is a lawyer who the president appoints to provide advice on all issues concerning the president and the administration.)

The lawyer's assistant said Hunt was not there, but he might be at a public relations firm where he worked as a writer. Woodward called the firm, and Hunt finally came on the line. Woodward asked why Hunt's name was in a Watergate burglar's address book. Hunt hung up.

Woodward called Hunt's boss at the PR firm. He suggested that Hunt's previous work with the CIA might be the reason his name was coming up. Woodward could now see a connection among key players: there could be a thread from the burglars to the White House, via Hunt, an old CIA connection, and the president's special counsel. However, this seemed like a possibly weak connection. "Anyone could have someone's name in an address book," Woodward wrote years later in the *Washington Post*. "I wanted to be careful about guilt by association." However, he was intrigued enough that he ignored Felt's earlier request that he leave him alone at the office. He called Felt again.

This time, Felt answered his question, though he said his answer had to be off the record. That meant that Woodward could not print the information. Even though Woodward could not use what Felt said, it could be a useful clue for Woodward's investigation. Woodward could use the information to try to learn more from other people. Felt told Woodward that Hunt was a prime suspect in the burglary for many reasons.

In July, Bernstein traveled to Miami, Florida. Four of the five burglars had come from there. He "ingeniously," Woodward wrote, found a local lawyer and detective who had copies of a $25,000 check that had been deposited in one of the burglars' personal bank accounts. This was important because the check had been earmarked for Nixon's reelection campaign. A donor had given the check to Nixon's chief fundraiser. On August 1, the *Post* printed a

Woodward and Bernstein article that was the first to tie the White House, via Nixon's campaign fund, to Watergate.

A Complex Way to Meet

Woodward called Felt again at his office and then at his home. When Felt would not take his calls, Woodward showed up at his home. Woodward was desperate because no one else would talk with him. He said he and Bernstein had a list of everyone who worked for Nixon's reelection campaign. They were working their way down the list, trying to interview anyone on it. "We were getting lots of doors slammed in our faces" instead of answers, Woodward later wrote, along with "lots of frightened looks."

After Woodward showed up at Felt's home uninvited, Felt knew that Woodward would not take no for an answer. Felt ultimately agreed to talk with Woodward, but he said they had to be really careful. He remembered what he had learned from spies during World War II. He suggested a protocol, or series of steps that he and Woodward would have to follow to communicate safely with each other.

He told Woodward that he could watch the reporter's apartment regularly. In 1972, there was not a lot of security around apartment buildings. Anyone could drive down the alley that ran along Woodward's apartment. Woodward also figured that his balcony could be seen from dozens of nearby offices and other apartments.

If Woodward opened his curtains, Felt suggested, that meant he wanted a meeting. Woodward said he did not usually leave his curtains closed, so that idea would not work. They would need another signal. Woodward said he had a flowerpot on his balcony, and in that pot was a small, bright-red flag. The two men agreed that if Woodward moved the flowerpot from near the balcony's railing back toward his apartment, that was a signal that he needed to meet with Felt. They would meet that same night at 2:00 a.m. in an underground parking garage just over the Key Bridge.

Felt had further instructions that they would have to follow. When Woodward left his apartment for their meeting, he was to take the building's back stairs to the alley. He should not take his car but get a taxi. He should not take that taxi all the way to the parking garage. Instead, he should take it to a nearby hotel, walk a little bit, and then get in a second cab. He should ask the cab to let him off a few blocks from the garage. He should walk the rest of the way. All of this should take one to two hours.

Moving the flowerpot was the way Woodward told Felt he wanted a meeting. Now they needed to figure out a way for Felt to communicate with Woodward if he wanted a meeting. He asked the reporter about daily mail and other deliveries. Woodward said he had a subscription to the *Washington Post*, but Felt did not like that the paper was left outside Woodward's apartment door. Woodward's copy of the *New York Times* was left in the lobby of the apartment building—along with copies for a number of the other tenants. Woodward's copy was marked with his unit number, 617. Felt said he could get to the newspaper and mark it with a code: he would circle page 20, and he would draw the hands of a clock indicating a meeting time in the same parking garage.

The Importance of Sources

At one point, Woodward apologized to Felt for pestering him. Felt admitted he wanted to be Woodward and Bernstein's source. He had been on the other side, too,

Bob Woodward signaled Mark Felt, also known as Deep Throat, from the bottom balcony shown here.

Watergate's Stories

asking questions, because the FBI also relied on volunteer informants. He understood the pressure the journalists were under.

Woodward later wrote that he had noticed that Felt's generosity was unusual. However, when you're an investigative journalist, you can have stories that are "enticing, complex, competitive and fast-breaking," Woodward said in a 2005 *Washington Post* article. At those times, all a journalist cares about is whether or not the information checks out as true. "We were swimming, really living, in the fast-moving rapids," Woodward wrote of investigating and writing about Watergate. "There was no time to ask why [informants] were talking or whether they had an ax to grind."

Bernstein never met with Felt during the investigation. The in-person meetings were restricted to Woodward and Felt only. However, according to Woodward, Bernstein was instrumental in cultivating, finding, earning the trust of, and encouraging other sources to talk to the two investigative journalists. Woodward told NPR in 2014 that "the key to their reporting was the way they approached conversations with sources." According to Woodward, Bernstein was instrumental in developing that approach. They would visit potential sources at their homes after work, "when they're relaxed, when there are no press people around. When the time is limitless to a certain extent and you're there saying, 'Help me. I need your help,' which are the most potent words in journalism. And people will kind of unburden themselves, or at least tell part of the story."

Seymour Hersh would start reporting on Watergate for the *New York Times* about seven months after the Watergate burglary. In a 2005 article for the *New Yorker*, he wrote that anonymous sources were "essential" to journalists investigating Watergate. They were the main reason the president was unable to stop the story or spin it in his favor.

Hersh said members of congressional investigating committees, the Justice Department, and even the Nixon administration were all discreetly giving reporters information. They did this because they were "outraged by the sheer bulk and gravity of the corrupt activities" of the White House. They were horrified by what they witnessed. They also were horrified because they themselves were betrayed. They were charged with maintaining national security, yet they were being taped against their will. As Hersh said, they wondered what else they did not realize was happening. The country had never experienced anything like this. People were genuinely scared that the president was about to do something extreme to hold on to his power or that the government was about to crumble entirely.

This meant that there was a steady stream of information. The information was also timely. If the president was upset about allegations a newspaper made about him, the reporter received from a high-level source confidential transcripts of the president's actual words. The very next day, the newspaper could publish those previously confidential transcripts.

Hersh did not know that Felt was so important to Woodward and Bernstein's reporting. He knew Felt was talking to the press. However, he thought Felt was talking to a colleague of Hersh's at the *Times*. He also believed that Woodward and Bernstein's information came from a variety of sources. (Good investigative journalists do not often rely on just one source.)

Hersh did know that he shared at least one anonymous informant with the *Washington Post* duo of Woodward and Bernstein. He explained in the *New Yorker* how he learned that. Hersh visited a source he thought was giving information only to him. He found a handwritten note on the informant's office door that said, "Kilroy Was Here." Woodward was known to leave such a mark.

Watergate, Part II

The *New York Times* hired Hersh in December 1972 to cover the Watergate beat. According to Hersh's *New Yorker* article recalling his work covering Watergate, the *Times* had been "overwhelmed" by Woodward and Bernstein's reporting for the past several months. In his newly created role at the *Times*, Hersh was just "trying to catch up."

Even once it became clear that the *Washington Post* would be publishing at least an article a day on Watergate, the *New York Times* did not assign a reporter to the unfolding story. Henry Kissinger, President Nixon's national security adviser, had told the newspaper that the Watergate story could not ultimately connect directly to the White House. So, the *New York Times* focused on Vietnam. This was a justifiable move, in some ways. Covering the unpopular war, which included plenty of military and government missteps and cover-ups, was also investigative journalism at its most important.

One of Hersh's first Watergate stories was on hush money paid directly from Nixon's reelection campaign to the burglars. As soon as it was published, Hersh remembered, "Woodward and Bernstein got in touch with me and essentially welcomed me aboard."

According to the *Washington Post*, Hersh's scoop "helped restart" interest in Watergate. Everyone involved in exposing the government's wrongdoing was happy about that. Leonard Downie Jr. was an investigative journalist who began publishing articles in the *Washington Post* in the mid-1960s. He echoed what Hersh said. When the *Los Angeles Times* and CBS News, along with the *New York Times*, finally started providing regular Watergate coverage at the end of 1972, it was "almost welcome competition." Woodward and Bernstein, along with their *Post* support reporters, including Downie, had been at times ignored, doubted, and attacked for what they were publishing. "It was a tense time," Downie wrote years later in the *Washington Post*, "with our credibility and our newspaper's future on the line."

Reporting on, and Making, History

The only resignation of a sitting US president happened because five men broke into an office in 1972. That break-in became a career-destroying scandal because investigative journalists uncovered the answers to who was behind the break-in and why. Thanks to reporters like Woodward, Bernstein, and Hersh, and sources like Felt, United States history was changed forever, as was journalism. This second golden era of investigative reporting at the end of the twentieth century prepared the field for what would come in the new millennium.

Journalists still debate big issues, like these reporters did at a PBS-sponsored panel discussion about terrorism in 2011.

Investigative Journalism Half a Century After Watergate

The twenty-first century is ripe for investigative journalism just like the early 1970s were. There is political and social change. People are interested in following developing news stories. Technology allows people to learn updates even in the middle of night while in bed.

"Woodward and Bernstein's role remains crucial," Leonard Downie Jr. wrote for the *Washington Post* in 2012. "We continue to live in perilous times, making investigative journalism as essential to our democracy as the Watergate stories were." Downie is keenly aware of what might have happened had those two reporters, and their colleagues, not cut through the metaphorical weeds to find a trail between the Watergate burglary and the White House.

In his 2012 article, Downie noted how investigative reporting in his home newspaper helped reduce police shootings in Washington, DC. Journalists served as watchdogs to make sure that philanthropic, advocacy, and educational organizations used their donated money appropriately. Investigative articles exposed corruption in Congress and improved living conditions in medical centers for military veterans. In other words, the work of Nellie Bly, who investigated medical facilities, through David Halberstam and Seymour Hersh, who investigated war, through Woodward and Bernstein, who investigated government, has continued.

However, forty years after Watergate, Downie wondered if too many reporters were not looking for those trails in twenty-first-century events. "Perhaps the surest sign of the endurance and importance of Watergate-legacy investigative reporting is the questioning of whether the news media should have more aggressively and quickly exposed the underlying causes of recent national crises," Downie wrote.

Seymour Hersh wrote something similar in 2005 in the *New Yorker*. He said that Nixon and Kissinger both expressed confusion in their memoirs. They did not understand why the White House "could not do what it wanted, at home or in Vietnam." The reason it could not, Hersh wrote, is "just as valid today." The people demanded they follow the rules of the country's democracy and Constitution. "That is the legacy of Watergate."

Inspiring Future Journalists

Many journalism students have been inspired by Woodward and Bernstein's book *All the President's Men*, as well as the movie based on the book. Because Woodward and Bernstein became famous, other investigative journalists have also become "marketable brand names." Downie suggested in 2012 that today's students are not just dreaming of fame but learning solid skills. They are learning reporting techniques that Woodward and Bernstein made "central to the ethos of investigative reporting." Downie offered this advice to rising investigative journalists: "Become an expert on your subject. Knock on doors to talk to sources in person. Protect the confidentiality of sources when necessary. Never rely on a single source. Find documents. Follow the money. Pile one hard-won detail on top of another until a pattern becomes discernible." According to Downie, those very techniques, made legendary by Woodward and Bernstein, helped investigative journalist Dana Priest reveal in 2005 that the CIA was using secret prisons outside the United States to hold and interrogate suspected terrorists.

Downie suggested that television programs like *60 Minutes* would not exist if not for the Watergate coverage. That program features investigative journalism. Citizen journalists also have found a place in investigative journalism because of Woodward and Bernstein. Downie linked them within the long chain of investigative reporting. He wrote in the *Washington Post* that "crowdsourcing contributions and tweets … have sometimes become the leading edge of the next investigative story." For example, the first reports of the Arab Spring, protests in the Middle East and North Africa in 2010 and 2011, came over Twitter. The tweets were written by everyday people acting as reporters. People turned to Twitter to learn what was happening. Even people who did not normally rely on Twitter for news went there to watch this story unfold. The

"-Gate": The Suffix of a Scandal

The Watergate scandal received that name because the burglary took place in the mixed-use development of offices, apartments, and a hotel that was named Watergate. At the time, "-gate" was simply part of the name of a place. Now, "-gate" has a different meaning. It has been used as a suffix, or ending part of a word, to mean "scandal," "cover-up," or "unethical behavior."

According to the *Chicago Tribune*, the *National Lampoon* magazine was the first to use "-gate" in this way, in 1973. William Safire, who was a conservative *New York Times* columnist (as well as a language enthusiast), has been credited with coining at least twenty "-gates." He made many of them about events that happened during the term of President Jimmy Carter, a liberal. Before becoming a journalist, Safire was President Nixon's speech writer. He admitted to historian and writer Eric Alterman that he "may have been seeking to minimize the importance of the crimes committed by his former boss with this silliness." By calling everything a "-gate," he tried to lessen the negative weight of the Watergate scandal.

Now it is used in politics, sports, entertainment, and every other industry. The Merriam-Webster dictionary added a definition of "-gate" in 1993. When Facebook founder Mark Zuckerberg wore a sweatshirt to meet with investors in 2012, and the meeting did not go well, the media began calling it "Hoodiegate." Kory Stamper, an editor with Merriam-Webster, acknowledges that "the force of [-gate's] meaning has certainly changed over the years."

Journalist William Safire coined many terms using the suffix "-gate."

Martha Brockenbrough, founder of the Society for the Promotion of Good Grammar, says that the common, widespread, and perhaps overzealous use of "-gate" in this way is "a real Usagegate."

American Press Institute explained in a 2014 study that "the majority of Americans across generations now combine a mix of sources and technologies to get their news."

CIJ and the IRE

After the explosive headlines of Watergate, as well as those of other major world events, investigative journalists in both Canada and the United States started professional organizations. In Canada, the group was called the Centre for Investigative Journalism (CIJ). In the United States, it was called Investigative Reporters and Editors (IRE).

Centre for Investigative Journalism

The CIJ formed in 1978. It all began with a conversation between two investigative journalists early that year. Henry Aubin had just published a book, *City for Sale*. It was a piece of investigative journalism. Jock Ferguson was an investigative reporter who was reviewing Aubin's book. When they met to talk, they both expressed frustration at how lonely their jobs were. Even in this golden age of investigative journalism, they did not have a lot of colleagues. It would always be scary for newspaper publishers and television editors to hire investigative reporters. Those journalists exposed corruption at the highest levels of society. The people behind that wrongdoing had the money and the power to cause real problems for newspapers and television stations.

Aubin and Ferguson immediately talked two other investigative journalists into joining them. By October 1978, fifty people had paid membership dues. Fifty more had expressed interest in learning more about the CIJ. They planned a convention. They hoped for 150 people to attend. When the day arrived, 350 people attended.

By 1990, the name had changed to the Canadian Association of Journalists (CAJ). Many of the members disagreed with this name change. They felt it would take the focus away from investigative journalism, which was the reason the organization had formed in the first place. The members who argued for the name change wanted more inclusivity. They wanted reporters of all types to feel welcome in the organization. This was another example of how investigative journalism continues to rise and fall in popularity.

Investigative Reporters and Editors

IRE began in 1975. Like the CIJ in Canada, IRE started because investigative journalists in the United States wanted community. They wanted to be able to share story ideas, investigating and reporting techniques, and sources. They wanted to improve the quality of investigative journalism and elevate it in the public's perception.

Also like the CIJ, IRE started small but grew quickly. Four people organized the IRE's first meeting. From Indiana, Myrta Pulliam and Harley Bierce were part of the *Indianapolis Star*'s Pulitzer Prize–winning investigative team. Paul Williams was former managing editor of Sun Newspapers in Omaha, Nebraska, and had worked on journalistic exposés. Ron Koziol was the fourth founding member. He covered police and courts for the *Chicago Tribune* in Illinois. Fourteen people attended that first meeting. A year later, three hundred attended the first IRE conference.

At the conference, the group selected a name. Columnist Les Whitten suggested that the basic definition of an investigative journalist was someone who expressed "a sense of outrage." Investigative reporters were angry because of wrongdoing. They told the stories of people who were angry, and their stories made people angry. The first letters of Investigative Reporters and Editors spell the word "ire," which means "anger."

The conference was significant beyond the naming of the group. The attendees agreed not to accept funding from organizations or people outside of journalism. They did not want anyone with money to think they could control what stories the reporters wrote. They also did not want to become corrupt—that would be exactly what they fought against as investigative journalists!

It was also impressive that this group of individuals had succeeded in organizing themselves at all. This had not been done before. Until then, investigative journalists had worked in isolation. They worked by themselves because

There were more people than seats at the Investigative Reporters and Editors Annual Conference in 2005.

they were forced to and because they chose to. Many media outlets did not hire more than one investigative journalist. Also, because their work could be dangerous and could lead them to question whom they could trust, many journalists

Investigative Journalism Half a Century After Watergate **83** had difficulty opening up to others. They were pleasantly surprised they worked so well together. "It was exciting, it was fun, it was interesting," Myrta Pulliam, Pulitzer Prize winner and IRE cofounder, later said of the meeting where they planned the conference. "Everybody had their own idea of what that is, and we had to mush all of that into something that would work."

Because of this camaraderie, IRE was able to mobilize its members to act as a unified group when tragedy struck, as it did in 1976 when a reporter was killed reporting a story and his colleagues helped to continue his work after his death. The Arizona Project, as this series of articles would come to be called, is a unique example of investigative journalism in the post-Watergate era because reporters from around the country voluntarily worked together to uncover a story.

The Arizona Project

The Arizona Project has been called a landmark moment of investigative reporting. Thirty-eight reporters and editors from newspapers around the country collaborated on a twenty-three-part series about organized crime in Arizona.

A Deadly Tip

Dan Bolles was an investigative reporter in Arizona. He received a phone call from a person claiming to be able to connect two prominent state leaders to the Mafia. Many people think of big cities like New York, Chicago, and Los Angeles when they think of the Mafia. That was exactly why Arizona was a Mafia hotspot in the 1970s. The state was relatively low in population. Phoenix was one of only two cities there. It was big enough to be interesting for

The death of Dan Bolles led to a unique series of investigative journalism stories.

the mob and small enough that law enforcement did not want to put resources there. As the IRE website explains, "An Arizonan's climb to power could be made with the handshake of a mobster."

For that reason, the tip Bolles received understandably interested him. He agreed to meet the caller. The man never showed up. Bolles returned to his car to go home. As he sat down in the driver's seat, a bomb under his car exploded.

The Start of the Arizona Project

Bolles had been scheduled to speak at the first IRE conference. His absence greatly affected the attendees. They mourned his death. They also knew that what happened to him could have happened to any one of them.

As a group, they made an interesting decision. They would go to Arizona and follow Bolles's leads. As the IRE website explains, they "went to prove a point and buy an investigative reporting insurance policy: You can't kill a story by killing a reporter."

They set up temporary headquarters in a hotel room in Phoenix. They replaced the beds and nightstands with file cabinets and desks. Bob Greene, a Pulitzer Prize–winning Newsday editor, was in charge of the project.

Interested reporters and editors from around the country took vacation or paid time off from their newspapers to work in Phoenix for a few weeks at a time. This project would end up lasting five months. They interviewed businesspeople, politicians, and mobsters. Bolles's tipster had implied that state leaders were involved in land fraud with the Mafia. So, the IRE members tracked down land-fraud documents as far away as Las Vegas. They cross-indexed and verified their findings.

An Example of the Journalists' Work

Harry Jones signed on for a three-week shift to help with the reporting. He worked as an investigative reporter for the *Kansas City Star* in Missouri. He had not known Bolles, but he had worked with Bolles's younger sister on their college newspaper.

His first assignment with the Arizona Project was to go to Arrowhead Ranch with a few other IRE members. Arrowhead was a citrus farm rumored to hire undocumented immigrants to harvest the fruit. Bob Goldwater was co-owner. He was one of Arizona's most important businesspeople. He was also the brother of Barry Goldwater, one of Arizona's US senators. Barry Goldwater was known for being a major and longstanding leader in Arizona. He had even run for president of the United States.

People suspected the Goldwater brothers of having connections to the Mafia. No one had proved that yet. Bolles had been trying to. His IRE colleagues were continuing his work. They wanted to prove even one illegality—like Bob Goldwater hiring people not allowed to work in the United States. They hoped that would spiral into further revelations.

Jones and the other IRE members arrived at the farm, which was a half-hour drive north of Phoenix. They parked their two cars. Their first task was getting onto the property without being seen by security guards or the helicopter they heard flying in slow circles above them.

Jones avoided being caught as he ran through the trees. He came upon a group of workers resting in shelters made from crates normally used to transport oranges. The flies were thick. The farm did not provide toilets for the workers.

Jones asked the workers if they had identification cards. They said that of course they had IDs. They showed Jones.

He knew immediately they were fake. The workers did not know they were fake. The coyotes, or guides, who had helped them cross the border from Mexico had lied to them. Arrowhead Ranch had hired them even though they also knew these IDs were fake.

Revealing these illegal hiring practices was one of the first articles the reporters of the Arizona Project published. Its series of articles on political corruption in Arizona debuted on March 13, 1977.

Flaws of the Arizona Project

The Arizona Project was not a utopia for all investigative reporters. For example, there was discrimination based on gender. Myrta Pulliam cofounded IRE. She also had won a Pulitzer Prize when she was only in her twenties. She had been part of the prizewinning *Indianapolis Star* team that investigated police corruption. She was equal to or more experienced than her male colleagues on the Arizona Project. Yet they asked her to make the coffee when the office pot in their temporary Phoenix office ran low. Pulliam knew that refusing would not solve the issue quickly. So, she made the coffee—by dumping a lot of grounds into the coffeemaker and making it so strong that it was undrinkable. "They never asked me to make coffee again," she said on the IRE website.

The Arizona Project also suffered from some negative perceptions of it. Prominent news organizations such as the *Washington Post* and the *New York Times* refused to allow their reporters to help. They said, according to the IRE website, that the Arizona Project was promoting sensationalism and vigilante journalism. They thought

IRE was being overly dramatic. They also thought those reporters would hurt the industry by working freelance.

The Arizona Project also almost bankrupted IRE. A rancher with Mafia connections sued IRE for libel. The jury sided with the reporters; the court said the reporters had not libeled the rancher. However, they also awarded the rancher $15,000 for emotional stress. This encouraged others to also sue the reporters. Five others named in Arizona Project articles also sued. Juries continued to award them money that IRE had to pay.

Staying Power

IRE had a tumultuous first few years. It spearheaded the Arizona Project, which was considered a landmark, or important, moment for investigative journalism. It also faced debt because of lawsuits and had to keep moving its headquarters. After all of that, it continues to exist. It has staying power despite these challenges. More than five thousand investigative journalists and editors are members, according to IRE's website. It has even directly inspired other investigative collaborations. IRE gives one example on its website. When reporter Khadija Ismahilova was arrested and jailed in Azerbaijan, her fellow journalists continued her work.

A Different World for Investigative Journalism

In many ways, investigative journalism since Watergate has been affected by forces outside its control. The world is a different place than it was half a century ago. There are two major factors in the changing landscape of investigative journalism: funding and technology.

Finding Funding

According to Leonard Downie's 2012 *Washington Post* editorial, "Dramatic shifts in audience and advertising revenue have undermined the financial model that subsidized so much investigative reporting" during the late twentieth century. Newspapers want to continue to cover big stories, but they don't have the staff to do so. Television stations may lean on consumer protection investigations in order to increase ratings. For example, they may investigate illegal sales tactics by telemarketers, companies not following their advertised warranties for broken products, or outrageous service fees by banks. These can be important stories to people's lives, but they are not the investigative stories of Woodward and Bernstein's time.

The gap has been filled in part by nonprofit, internet-based investigative reporting organizations. Journalists who used to work for newspapers or television have left those jobs to start news sites like ProPublica, based in New York City; the Texas Tribune in Austin; California Watch, which works throughout the state; the Voice of San Diego, in Southern California; the Center for Public Integrity, out of Washington, DC; MinnPost in Minnesota; and the Center for Investigative Reporting, out of Berkeley, California. According to a 2013 study by the Pew Research Center, there were 174 nonprofit news sites such as those. All but nine states were home to at least one news site. About 21 percent focused on general investigative reporting. Another 17 percent investigated government. Thirteen percent reported on public and foreign affairs, while

38 percent focused on state-level issues and 29 percent on city-level concerns.

The *Atlantic* says ProPublica's investigative journalism "has set a remarkable standard for quality on a range of subjects." That quality comes at a steep cost. One two-year story, on the dangers of Tylenol's main ingredient, cost $750,000. Foundations, individuals, and sometimes journalism schools have been funding these sites. Bigger wallets need to step up, the *Atlantic* argues. "Technology companies that have earned billions in a relatively few years could well afford to become backers of invaluable journalism that is one of the mainstays of their industry." Of course, then, investigative journalists will need to watch that they are not controlled by the businesses funding them. That was a fear IRE had in seeking funding for its work.

How Technology and Investigative Journalism Moved Forward Together

Newspaper reporting broke the Watergate story. Television, a major new technology of the early 1970s, solidified it in people's minds. Television shattered records covering the Watergate hearings, which were led by the Senate committee investigating Watergate. All three commercial networks—ABC, CBS, and NBC—and the noncommercial PBS televised the initial phase of the hearings, which lasted from May 17, 1973, through August 7, 1973. This totaled 319 hours of television, a record for coverage of a single event. According to the Museum of Broadcast Communications, one survey found that 85 percent of all US homes watched at least some of the hearings.

According to the book *The Journalism of Outrage*, it was the news coverage of those hearings that "finally made

The Heywood Broun Award

Bob Woodward and Carl Bernstein won the Heywood Broun Award in 1972, the year they broke the Watergate story. The mission of the award is to "recognize individual journalistic achievement by members of the working media, particularly if it helps right a wrong or correct an injustice."

The award was named for journalist Heywood Broun. He was a columnist for newspapers in New York from 1912 until the year he died, 1939. He also wrote for the *Nation*, the *New Republic*, and *Harper's*, among other publications. He was one of the founders of the American Newspaper Guild. He served as its first president, starting in 1933.

According to the NewsGuild–Communications Workers of America, he "was a passionate champion of the underdog and the disadvantaged." They write that Broun believed reporters "could help right wrongs, especially social ills."

In 2016, journalist Terrence McCoy, who worked for the *Washington Post*, just as Woodward and Bernstein did, won the Heywood Broun Award. McCoy uncovered the story of companies making money off the lead-poisoning of people, most of whom were poor and black.

Heywood Broun's contributions to journalism are remembered with the Heywood Broun Award.

Investigative Journalism Half a Century After Watergate **93**

Watergate a widely credible public issue." According to an October 1972 Gallup poll, four months into Woodward and Bernstein's reporting, only 52 percent of Americans recognized the word "Watergate." On November 7, five months into the reporting, Nixon was reelected by one of the widest Electoral College margins in history—his opponent, George McGovern, won only the state of Massachusetts and the District of Columbia. Today, we credit the early newspaper coverage of Watergate with taking down a president. However, we know it did not do that singlehandedly or immediately. Yet because of it, *The Journalism of Outrage* says, "the groundwork was being laid for a new form of media competition that ultimately helped to advance" the Watergate story and future stories.

IRE provides just one example of how journalism continues to adapt to changing times. In the late twentieth century and early twenty-first century, IRE has "played a role in the evolving definition of investigative reporting" to include technology. In 1992, Brant Houston took over the Missouri Institute for Computer-Assisted Reporting. Now called the National Institute for Computer-Assisted Reporting, this organization trains journalists in finding and analyzing electronic information. In 1997, Houston became president of IRE. With one person leading both organizations, they effectively merged. Journalists have seen this as a positive thing. "Databases and journalism go hand in hand," Houston says. "Once you blend these things together, investigative reporting can have a much greater impact."

The Watergate Effect

Decades after the second golden age of investigative journalism of the late 1960s and early 1970s, people still debate which big story ushered in the new era, how that work has changed journalism today, and even how to define investigative journalism. Did reporting of Vietnam or reporting of Watergate restart investigative journalism? Are citizen journalists part of the investigative legacy? Who will fund investigative reports in the future, and how will that affect the bias of journalists taking that payment?

What is certain is that government leaders, all the way up to the president of the United States, have been brought to justice because of the swipe of a journalist's pen or the tap of the reporter's keyboard. The more complex and accessible technology gets, the more readily stories will reach around the world, revealing more secrets for more people. Finally, what is most certain is that the public plays a crucial role in allowing investigative journalism to flourish. People have to want to learn what journalists uncover. People must care about there being a response to what is learned. And people need to support unbiased news outlets to produce and publish critical pieces of investigative journalism.

Chronology

1887 Nellie Bly's *Ten Days in a Mad-House* is published.

1906 President Theodore Roosevelt introduces the word "muckraker" to the public.

1943 Bob Woodward is born.

1944 Carl Bernstein is born.

ca. 1945–1991 The United States participates in the Cold War.

1950 McCarthyism begins.

1951 Edward R. Murrow's *See It Now* television show debuts.

1963 Jessica Mitford's book *The American Way of Death* is published; Katharine Graham becomes publisher of the *Washington Post* and one of the most important women in the world.

1964 The United States becomes directly involved in the Vietnam War; David Halberstam earns a Pulitzer Prize for his Vietnam reporting.

1969 Jack Anderson takes over the Washington Merry-Go-Round column.

1970 Seymour Hersh wins a Pulitzer Prize for his work reporting on the 1968 My Lai Massacre and the government cover-up of the massacre.

1971 The *Washington Post* publishes the Pentagon Papers.

1972 The Watergate scandal begins with a burglary; Bob Woodward and Carl Bernstein begin reporting on Watergate for the *Washington Post*; Jack Anderson wins a Pulitzer Prize for his reporting on US government involvement in the Indo-Pakistan War.

1973 The Watergate hearings are televised; the *Washington Post* wins a Pulitzer Prize for its Watergate coverage.

1974 Richard Nixon becomes the first US president to resign; *All the President's Men* is published.

1976 *All the President's Men* becomes a movie.

2005 Deep Throat reveals his true name, Mark Felt.

Glossary

beat The subject, event, or person that a journalist is assigned to cover.

break The journalist who publishes the first story about an event "breaks" it.

Cold War The state of political hostility without active warfare between the Soviet Union and the United States that lasted from about 1945 to 1991.

corruption Dishonest or fraudulent conduct by those in power.

exposé A journalistic report that reveals the facts of a scandal.

freelancer A journalist who researchers and writes a story and then tries to sell it to any number of media outlets; a freelance journalist is not on staff at one publication or television station.

golden age Peak time for something; the time when it is at its height of popularity or influence.

informant Someone who provides information to another person.

muckraking Used negatively, it means someone is looking for damaging information to cause trouble unnecessarily; many investigative journalists over the decades have proudly called themselves "muckrakers."

New Journalism This form of reporting, popular in the 1960s and 1970s, combines journalistic research with fiction's storytelling techniques.

scoop A piece of news published by a newspaper or broadcast by a television or radio station before its rivals publish or broadcast it.

source A person who provides information to someone else.

spin To attempt to influence the public's impression of a story, often by trying to cast it in a favorable light.

tip A reliable piece of inside information.

Further Information

Books

Gaines, Ann Graham. *Richard M. Nixon: Our Thirty-Seventh President.* Mankato, MN: The Child's World, 2015.

Graham, Katharine. *Personal History.* New York: Vintage, 1998.

Hall, Homer L., and Logan H. Aimone. *High School Journalism.* New York: Rosen Publishing, 2009.

Tracy, Kathleen. *The Watergate Scandal.* Hallandale, FL: Mitchell Lane Publishers, 2007.

Woodward, Bob, and Carl Bernstein. *All the President's Men.* New York: Simon & Schuster, 1974.

Websites

Carl Bernstein
http://www.carlbernstein.com/home.php

Explore photos, articles, and a profile of Carl Bernstein on his official website.

IRE
https://www.ire.org

Learn more about Investigative Reporters and Editors and how to get involved.

The *Washington Post*: Watergate
https://www.washingtonpost.com/politics/watergate

Find a comprehensive look at the reporting of the Watergate scandal from the newspaper that broke the story.

Bob Woodward
http://bobwoodward.com/

Investigative journalist Bob Woodward's site provides a wealth of information about the journalist and his stories.

Videos

"President Nixon Resigns – August 9, 1974"
https://www.youtube.com/watch?v=NogWhoE418k

Watch footage of Watergate reporting in this video from NBC News Archives.

"So You Want to Be an Investigative Journalist?"
https://www.youtube.com/watch?v=bgHo6XgDqcA

Journalism.co.uk, a resource website for journalists, reveals the exciting and the challenging aspects of being an investigative journalist.

"Tips from Bob Woodward on Investigative Journalism"
https://www.youtube.com/watch?v=VVKGUctuoXE

In this video by the *Washington Post*, Bob Woodward discusses how journalists got information before the digital age and how they get information today.

Bibliography

Alterman, Eric. *Sound and Fury: The Making of the Punditocracy*. Ithaca, NY: Cornell University Press, 1999.

Biography.com. "Carl Bernstein." Last updated October 28, 2015. https://www.biography.com/people/carl-bernstein-102815.

———. "Edward R. Murrow." Last updated April 27, 2017. https://www.biography.com/people/edward-r-murrow-9419104.

———. "Mark Felt Biography." Last updated September 29, 2017. https://www.biography.com/people/william-mark-felt-396780.

Burkeman, Oliver. "Scoop." *Guardian*, October 8, 2004. https://www.theguardian.com/books/2004/oct/09/pulitzerprize.awardsandprizes.

Carberry, Belinda. "The Revolution in Journalism with an Emphasis on the 1960's and 1970's." Yale-New Haven Teachers Institute. Retrieved November 1, 2017. http://teachersinstitute.yale.edu/curriculum/units/1983/4/83.04.05.x.html.

Chisholm, Anne. "Obituary: Jessica Mitford." *Independent*, July 24, 1996. http://www.independent.co.uk/news/obituaries/obituary-jessica-mitford-1330361.html.

C-SPAN. "Watergate and Political Cartoonists." June 12, 1997. https://www.c-span.org/video/?86675-1/watergate-political-cartoonists&start=230.

Dews, Fred, and Thomas Young. "Ten Noteworthy Moments in U.S. Investigative Journalism." Brookings, October 20, 2014. https://www.brookings.edu/blog/brookings-now/2014/10/20/ten-noteworthy-moments-in-u-s-investigative-journalism.

Downie, Leonard, Jr. "Forty Years After Watergate, Investigative Journalism Is at Risk." *Washington Post*, June 7, 2012. https://www.washingtonpost.com/opinions/forty-years-after-watergate-investigative-journalism-is-at-risk/2012/06/07/gJQArTzILV_story.html?utm_term=.d00f3caf4921.

Economist. "Katharine Graham." July 19, 2001. http://www.economist.com/node/699638.

Fair, Julia. "Bob Woodward on Trump's Presidency: 'This Is a Test' for the Media." *USA Today*, November 14, 2017. https://www.usatoday.com/story/news/politics/2017/11/14/bob-woodward-trumps-presidency-this-test-media/863917001.

Fakazis, Liz. "New Journalism." *Encyclopaedia Britannica*, March 28, 2016. https://www.britannica.com/topic/New-Journalism.

Farhi, Paul. "The Ever-Iconoclastic, Never-to-Be-Ignored, Muckraking Seymour Hersh." *Washington Post*, May 15, 2015. https://www.washingtonpost.com/lifestyle/style/the-ever-iconoclastic-never-to-be-ignored-muckraking-seymour-hersh/2015/05/15/4eb1195a-f9a2-11e4-9ef4-1bb7ce3b3fb7_story.html?utm_term=.25e91a65ca99.

Feeney, Mark. "*All the President's Men* Is a Superhero Flick for Journalists." *Slate*, June 14, 2017. http://www.slate.com/articles/arts/conspiracy_thrillers/2017/06/all_the_president_s_men_made_woodward_and_bernstein_the_stuff_of_journalistic.html.

Garay, Ronald. "Watergate." Museum of Broadcast Communications. Retrieved November 1 2017. http://www.museum.tv/eotv/watergate.htm.

Haberman, Clyde. "David Halberstam, 73, Reporter and Author, Dies." *New York Times*, April 24, 2007. http://www.nytimes.com/2007/04/24/arts/24halberstam.html.

Hersh, Seymour M. "Watergate Days." *New Yorker*, June 13, 2005. https://www.newyorker.com/magazine/2005/06/13/watergate-days.

Hodgson, Godfrey. "Katharine Graham." *Guardian*, July 18, 2001. https://www.theguardian.com/media/2001/jul/18/guardianobituaries.pressandpublishing.

Janssen, Kim. "Carl Bernstein: Russia Probe Feels 'Worse than Watergate.'" *Chicago Tribune*, November 2, 2017. http://www.chicagotribune.com/news/chicagoinc/ct-met-carl-bernstein-trump-1103-chicago-inc-20171101-story.html.

Kovacs, Kasia. "The History of IRE." IRE.org. Retrieved November 1, 2017. https://www.ire.org/about/history/#chapter2.

Kurtz, Howard. "Jack Anderson, Gentleman with a Rake." *Washington Post*, December 18, 2005. http://www.washingtonpost.com/wp-dyn/content/article/2005/12/17/AR2005121701223.html.

Manker, Rob. "After 40 Years, Can We Slam the Door on '-Gate' Already?" *Chicago Tribune*, May 29, 2012. http://articles.chicagotribune.com/2012-05-29/news/ct-talk-gate-words-manker-0529-20120529_1_scandal-nixon-speechwriter-william-safire.

Mari, Will. "Midcentury Cartoons for Worried Print Journalists." *Slate*, August 10, 2015. http://www.slate.com/blogs/the_vault/2015/08/10/history_of_journalism_cartoons_showing_anxieties_of_print_journalists_in.html.

Mitchell, Amy, Mark Jurkowitz, Jesse Holcomb, Jodi Enda, and Monica Anderson. "Nonprofit Journalism: A Growing but Fragile Part of the U.S. News System." Pew Research Center, June 10, 2013. http://www.journalism.org/2013/06/10/nonprofit-journalism.

NewsGuild–Communications Workers of America. "Heywood Broun Award." Retrieved November 1, 2017. http://www.newsguild.org/mediaguild3/?page_id=5429.

Newman, Judith. "The American Way of Death Revisited." *New York Times*, October 4, 1998. http://www.nytimes.com/books/98/10/04/bib/981004.rv115616.html.

NPR. "40 Years On, Woodward and Bernstein Recall Reporting on Watergate." *Morning Edition*, June 13, 2014. https://www.npr.org/2014/06/13/321316118/40-years-on-woodward-and-bernstein-recall-reporting-on-watergate.

Osnos, Peter. "These Journalists Spent Two Years and $750,000 Covering One Story." *Atlantic*, October 2, 2013. https://www.theatlantic.com/national/archive/2013/10/these-journalists-spent-two-years-and-750-000-covering-one-story/280151.

Pérez-Peña, Richard. "2 Ex-Timesmen Say They Had a Tip on Watergate First." *New York Times*, May 24, 2009. http://www.nytimes.com/2009/05/25/business/media/25watergate.html.

Protess, David L., Fay Lomax Cook, Jack C. Doppelt, James S. Ettema, Margaret T. Gordon, Donna R. Leff, and Peter Miller. *The Journalism of Outrage: Investigative Reporting and Agenda Building in America*. New York: The Guilford Press, 1991.

Roberts, Sam. "Anne Morrissy Merick, a Pioneer from Yale to Vietnam, Dies at 83." *New York Times*, May 9, 2017. https://www.nytimes.com/2017/05/09/business/media/anne-morrissy-merick-dead-abc-journalist-in-vietnam.html.

Sifry, Micah L. "Watergate and the Internet: A Cautionary Tale from Bob Woodward." *Techpresident*, April 10, 2012. http://techpresident.com/news/22031/watergate-and-internet-cautionary-tale-bob-woodward.

Spector, Ronald H. "The Vietnam War and the Media." *Encyclopaedia Britannica*, April 27, 2016. https://www.britannica.com/topic/The-Vietnam-War-and-the-media-2051426.

Sullivan, Patricia. "Investigative Columnist Jack Anderson Dies." *Washington Post*, December 18, 2005. http://www.washingtonpost.com/wp-dyn/content/article/2005/12/17/AR2005121701112.html.

Woodward, Bob. "How Mark Felt Became 'Deep Throat.'" *Washington Post*, June 20, 2005. https://www.washingtonpost.com/politics/how-mark-felt-became-deep-throat/2012/06/04/gJQAlpARIV_story.html.

Index

Page numbers in **boldface** are illustrations.

All the President's Men (book), 38, 44, 76–77
All the President's Men (film), 44–45, **45**, 77
Anderson, Jack, 27, **28**, 29–31, 49
Arab Spring, 77
Arizona Project, 84, 86–89

beat, 60, 72
Bernstein, Carl
    awards and praise, 31, 92
    biography, 33
    opinions, 35
    Watergate reporting, 57, 60, 62, 64–67, 70–73
Bly, Nellie, 12–13, **13**, 76
Bolles, Dan, 84, **85**, 86–87
break, 10, 14, 33, 36, 54, 70
Broun, Heywood, 92, **93**

Capote, Truman, 11
cartoons, 15–16, 24–25, 54–55, **55**
Centre for Investigative Journalism (CIJ), 80–81

CIA, 29–31, 56–57, 60, 65–66, 77
citizen journalists, 77, 95
civil rights movement, 10–11, 20, 54
Cold War, 10

Dean, John, 62
disillusionment, 10
Downie, Leonard, Jr., 7, 72–73, 75–77, 90

exposé, 8, 13, 20, 81

FBI, 32, 36–38, 43, 60, 70
Felt, Mark ("Deep Throat"), 31–33, 36–38, **37**, 41, 65–68, 70–71, 73
Freedom of Information Act, 15
freelancer, 21, 52, 89
funeral industry, 24

golden age, 6, 54, 73, 80, 94
Goldwater, Barry, 64, 87
Graham, Katharine, **26**, 38, **39**, 40–41, 49
Gray, L. Patrick, **42**, 43, 46

Halberstam, David, 20–21, 76
Hersh, Seymour, 14, 46, **47**, 48–49, 51–53, 70–73, 76
Hunt, E. Howard, 60, 65–66

Index **109**

impeachment, 63–64
Indianapolis Star, 81, 88
Indo-Pakistan War, 30
informant, 70–72
internet, 58–59, 77, 90
Investigative Reporters and Editors (IRE), 14, 80–84, 86–89, 91, 94
investigative reporting
   after Watergate, 75–77, 80–84, 86–91, 94
   definition of, 5, 81–82
   in 1950s–1960s, 16–17, 20–21, 24, 27
   in Progressive Era, 6, 8, 10, 12–13
   support for, 15, 90–91
   television and, 16, 77, 90
   Vietnam and, 11, 20–21, 51–53, 72
   Watergate as model of, 6–7, 20, 31, 51, 76–77

Kennedy, John F., 10, 20
Kilpatrick, Carroll, 62–64
Kissinger, Henry, 41, 72, 76

Lardner, George, Jr., 62
Lewis, Alfred E., 56–57
Lewis, Sinclair, 8, 10
libel, 15, 89
Liddy, G. Gordon, 60

McCarthy, Joseph, **9**, 20
McCord, James W., Jr., 60
Meyer, Lawrence, 60, 62
Mitchell, John, 60
Mitford, Jessica, 21, **22–23**, 24
muckraking, 5, 8, 10, 14, 24, 38, 48
Murrow, Edward R., 17, 20
My Lai Massacre, 51–53, **53**

New Journalism, 11, 14
New York Times, 14, 20–21, 24, 31, 43, 46, 48, 70–73, 78, 88
New York Times v. Sullivan, 15
Nixon, Richard, 6–7, **18**, 30, 41, 44, **50**, 52, 54, 60, **61**, 62–67, **63**, 71–72, 76, 78, 94

objectivity, 11, 14
organized crime, 84, 86–89

Pentagon Papers, 41
Phelps, Robert, 43, 46, 49
Priest, Dana, 77
ProPublica, 90–91
Pulitzer Prizes, 15, 21, 29–30, 33, 51, 53, 81, 84, 86, 88
Pulliam, Myrta, 81, 84, 88

Red Scare, 10, 17, 20, 24

Roosevelt, Theodore, 8, 10, 20

Safire, William, 78, **79**
scoop, 30, 49, 72
sensationalism, 88–89
60 Minutes, 77
Smith, Robert, 43, 46, 49
Society of Professional Journalists, 14–15
source, 27, 33, 36, 38, 58, 65, 68, 70–73, 77, 81
spin, 71
Steinem, Gloria, 11, 40

television, 6–7, 15–17, **18**, 19–21, 24, 41, 77, 80, 90–91
terrorism, 14, 33, 77
tip, 46, 52, 86
Trump, Donald, 34–35
Twitter, 77

Vietnam War, 11, 19–21, 41, 51–53, **53**, 55, 72, 76, 95

Washington Merry-Go-Round (column), 29–30
Washington Post, 7, 14, 27, 29–33, 36, 38, 40–41, 48–49, **50**, 56, 62–68, 70–73, 75, 77, 88, 90, 92

Watergate scandal
  aftermath, 6–7, 63–64, 73
  break-in, 56–57, 60, 64–67, 73
  cover-up, 43, 46, 62, 72
  cultural background of, 6–7, 10–11, 16, 51
  "Deep Throat" and, 36–38, 65–68, 70–71
  FBI investigation, 37, 60
  hearings, 7, **42**, 91
  legacy of, 7, 20, 58–59, 73, 76–79, 94–95
  reporting of, 14, 31, 48, 56–57, 60, 62–68, 70–73, 91, 94
Whitten, Les, 81–82
Wolfe, Tom, 11
women's rights movement, 10, 12–13
Woodward, Bob
  awards and praise, 31, 33, 92
  biography, 31–33
  Mark Felt and, 31–33, 65–68, 70–71
  opinions, 34–35, 58
  style, 14
  Watergate reporting, 57, 60, 62, 64–68, 70–73

About the Author

Kristin Thiel lives in Portland, Oregon, where she is a writer and editor of books, articles, and documents for publishers, individuals, and businesses. Thiel is the author of *The Fourth Estate: Television News and the 24-Hour News Cycle*. She has also worked on many of the books in the So, You Want to Be A… series, which offers career guidance for kids and is published by Beyond Words, an imprint of Simon & Schuster. She was the lead writer on a report for her city about funding for high school dropout prevention. Thiel has judged YA book contests and managed before-school and afterschool literacy programs for AmeriCorps VISTA.